Dedicated to the young ladies of
Creighton Court in Richmond, Virginia
and Sursum Corda neighborhood in Washington, D.C.

Never Forget

Never Forget

*The Riveting Story of One Woman's Journey
from Public Housing to the Corridors of Power*

Kay Coles James

With Jacquelline Cobb Fuller

ZondervanPublishingHouse
Grand Rapids, Michigan

A Division of HarperCollinsPublishers

NEVER FORGET
Copyright © 1992 by Kay Coles James

Requests for information should be addressed to:
Zondervan Publishing House
Grand Rapids, Michigan 49530

Library of Congress Cataloging-in-Publication Data

James, Kay Coles.
    Never forget : the riveting story of one woman's journey from the
    projects to the corridors of power / by Kay Coles James with
    Jacquelline Cobb Fuller.
       p. cm.
    ISBN 0-310-48200-3
    1. James, Kay Coles. 2. Afro-Americans—Biography. 3. National
Right to Life Committee (U.S.)—Biography. 4. Pro-life movement—
United States. 5. Abortion—United States. I. Fuller,
Jacquelline Cobb. II. Title.
E185.97.J33A3 1992
                                    323′.092—dc20 92–37115
                                                CIP

Edited by Lyn Cryderman

Printed in the United States of America

    93 94 95 96 / DH / 8 7 6 5 4 3 2

This edition is printed on acid-free paper and meets the American
National Standards Institute Z39.48 standard.

Contents

Foreword

E V E R Y S U M M E R I take my family back to the old Baltimore neighborhood in which I was raised. The primary reason is to see the folks and give my parents the annual opportunity of getting to know their grandchildren better. However, there is a second and equally important reason that I insist on this annual trip. It forces me to remember. As I canvass the neighborhood annually, it becomes vividly clear that I'm one of the fortunate ones. The knowledge that many of my friends are now dead, doped, and defeated, forces me to remember that the only reason I'm not among that number is the strong faith imparted to me by my parents, coupled with an almost obsessive commitment to family. I remember that while many of my contemporaries could stay out half the night, I had a curfew that had better be kept or else! I remember the family Bible studies and regular church attendance. I remember the spankings by Dad that kept me much more afraid of his wrath than the wrath of my peers. I remember my parents' praying that the Lord would send money for food so that we could eat and so that we could have enough oil to keep us warm. I remember tears in my dad's eyes when he had to rush me, his firstborn, to the hospital because I was dying with a massive asthma attack. I remember handing out Gospel tracts on the street corner while he preached to the masses passing by. I also remember going with him to prisons and nursing homes and having him say to me,

"Tony, you speak today."

The trip back home is not only for my benefit, however. It's also for the benefit of my children. As they see drug deals go down right in front of their eyes, I want them to learn that it was because of what I remember that they aren't faced with that environment day in and day out. I want them to know that it is because I remember the faith and family commitment my parents exhibited that they wake up daily to a mom and dad who have committed themselves to stay together no matter how tough the going gets. When they see their dad speaking before thousands of people, signing his books for ardent admirers, being seen and heard across the nation on national radio and TV, I want them to know that I remember that I am but a dwarf standing on the shoulders of giants.

A wise man once said that a people who lose track of their yesterday can have no meaningful tomorrow. The great tragedy of history is that men rarely learn from it. It is only as we learn from the successes and failures of those who have gone before us that we can wisely evaluate the present and plan properly for the future. Much of the aimlessness we see today in our culture at large and within the African-American community, in particular, testifies to the grim realities of what happens when societies begin to crumble because people lose track of what makes them strong.

It is precisely this reality that makes this book unique, so inspiring, so dynamic, and so timely. Out of the crucible of her own life and experience, Kay James vividly demonstrates the importance of *remembering*. At a time when many of our "cultural heroes" are known more for their failures than their successes; when our families are being ravaged by the erosion of values; when people seek meaning and identity in what they have and whom they know, it is refreshing and even transforming to be confronted with a hero of a different kind—one who defines reality by what God and family have molded her to be.

Kay James and those like her represent the hope for the twenty-first century—the only hope. For unlike many who exist only for the moment, these heroes recognize that the only way to having meaning for today and hope for tomorrow is to go "back to the future." The greatness of this work is not only that Kay lets us join her in a walk down her "memory lane," but even more important, she gives those who only want to forget or who have precious little to remember, the vicarious privilege of allowing the lessons of her life to serve as the foundation for new principles that should undergird and govern their own lives as well. They, too, then, can hold this book in one hand and their transformed lives in the other and say with confidence,

"I, too, will never forget!"

—Dr. Tony Evans

Founder and president of The Urban Alternative,
Former chaplain of the NFL Dallas Cowboys,
First black American to graduate with a doctoral degree
from Dallas Theological Seminary

chapter one

I WILL NEVER FORGET

IT WAS THE SUMMER of 1985 and the James Gang was on a mission. We had lived in the nation's capital for several years and had never taken time to do "the tourist thing." My husband, Charles, a manager with the phone company, expected to be transferred back to our hometown of Richmond, Virginia, so we decided to use every spare moment to show our children what a marvelous and historic city they had lived near but never seen. So here we were— Mom and Dad, eleven-year-old Chuck, ten-year-old Elizabeth, and seven-year-old Robbie—trying to cram every historic sight into a few weekends.

On this particular day, we were waiting in line to tour George Washington's home at Mount Vernon. It was hot and humid, Robbie had to go to the bathroom, and the other children were displaying that I'd-rather-be-shopping-at-an-air-conditioned-mall look. Robbie kept pestering us about finding a bathroom, so I finally tried to put him off by telling him that there were no bathrooms at Mount Vernon.

"There must be one someplace," he chafed. "George Washington had to pee, too."

"Robbie!" I scolded, noticing the family ahead of us.

We were a fairly even match: A dad reading the Mount
Vernon brochure, a mom standing with two or three grade-
school children, and a teenager who stayed near enough to
complain about the heat but far enough to retain an air of
adolescent indifference. They immediately picked up on
Robbie's brazen comment, pestering their parents with
questions about life in George Washington's day.

"Did he have any kids? Did they play football? Did they
ride horses?"

One question, however, caught my attention:

"How in the world did George mow all this lawn?" he
asked, gesturing to the seemingly endless stretch of grass
surrounding the main house.

It was a simple enough question, yet it held an
opportunity to lay open a great, neglected truth about some
of our founding fathers: These men who had fought so hard
and had sacrificed so much for the cause of liberty and
democracy, also owned slaves. George Washington, in fact,
once sold a slave to Thomas Jefferson. I feigned indifference
as I strained to hear how the mother would answer this
loaded question.

"Oh, I don't know," she sighed, "it must have taken
him a long time."

I was disappointed by her nonchalant reply. I was quite
sure that George Washington had never cut a blade of grass,
washed a dish, or cooked a meal in his life! If there ever was
a "teachable moment," this was it, and I decided to teach
more than my own family. I silently thanked the Lord for
my degree in African-American history and began to explain
in a voice loud enough to be heard by the family next to us.

"You know, kids, George Washington was a very
wealthy and powerful man in his time. In its heyday, the
Mount Vernon estate stretched out over 8000 acres. He
owned many slaves. There were around seventy-five who
worked here at Mount Vernon, and he owned many more
who worked on his four other farms. The slaves hunted and
fished for food; they cleaned the house and kept fires
burning; they tended the gardens, worked the fields. Slave

women spun flax and wool into cloth, and cooked and baked food in the kitchen. Some learned trades and made shoes and repaired saddles. We know that some slaves worked as carpenters and blacksmiths and built most of the buildings we're going to see today at Mount Vernon.

"Slaves also were responsible for the upkeep of this property, tending to the gardens, cutting the grass, caring for the livestock. In its day, Mount Vernon was known as one of the most regal mansions in America, and it was truly beautiful—but it was made beautiful on the backs of slaves.

"It was the sweat of your ancestors," I explained to my children, "that earned Mount Vernon its name. But unlike the gardeners and groundskeepers of today, they weren't allowed to receive financial reward for the work they had done. They were slaves."

I went on to explain that although he had held strong convictions about freedom, George Washington and most others of his era reserved these rights for white men. Women couldn't vote. Indians couldn't vote. Slaves couldn't vote. Only white men who owned land were entrusted with voting privileges in Virginia.

"It wasn't against the law then to own slaves," I said, mostly for the benefit of the kids in front of us inasmuch as my children knew that fact well enough. "George Washington had second thoughts later. He gave his slaves their freedom in his will. He also asked that the freed slaves be taught to read and write and be trained in a useful occupation."

My two older children, Chuck and Elizabeth, seemed to catch on to the significance of my history lesson. They nodded and looked out over the green grass and carefully manicured gardens. For them—and, I hoped, for the family ahead of us—the beauty of the estate took on a new meaning. What I hadn't expected was the impact it would have on me.

Robbie, on the other hand, wanted to know where the slaves went to the bathroom.

After touring the home, we wandered around the

property, down past the smokehouse, the wash house, and the stables. A lone cedar of Lebanon marked the path's turn into the woods. We followed the red brick path to the Washingtons' tomb, a sunlit and orderly arrangement of statues, vaulted arches and brick. We read the detailed descriptions on the tombs for George and Martha Washington and their family members buried alongside them.

For some reason, we decided to follow the path and then head to the next stop on our itinerary for that day. The red brick pathway soon turned to a loose gravel. The woods closed in around us. This was the stretch of path where they planted all the rebellious boxwoods that had outgrown their function as a decorative hedge. Here they were tree-size and wild, with trunks like spears. Their bushy tops formed a green canopy shielding us from the intense sun. The cool of the shade was rejuvenating on such a warm and sticky day.

The path emptied into a small circular clearing, with a short monument in its center. Elizabeth, our inquisitive one, was the first to discover the significance of the site by skipping ahead to see what we'd found.

"It's a slave tomb," she called back. "This is where they buried their slaves."

Off to the side, a marker told us where we were: *In memory of the Afro-Americans who served as slaves at Mount Vernon. This monument marking their burial ground, dedicated September 21, 1983: Mount Vernon Ladies Association.*

The cylinder-shaped marker sat on top of three concentric circles of brick, each one smaller and higher than its base. The circles were labeled *Faith; Hope;* and *Love* and *Love* was highest. There were no benches to offer a rest, so I sat on the brick retaining wall and stared at the simple memorial before me. Low and humble, it hovered close to the ground. No arches or vaults here. Its deep-woods feel and circular forms provided a sharp contrast to the pristine surroundings of the manor. Wild grasses and ivy crept in on the brick.

Charles sat down next to me in silence. He could tell that I was lost in thought. The kids were chasing each other around the edge of the brick circles, but I was too distracted to scold them. I thought about the slaves buried in the earth beneath me. My eyes fixed upon the lowest circle, *Faith*. *These were people of faith*, I mused.

My eyes glanced up the step to *Hope*. What was their hope? Did these illiterate slaves dare hope and dream about a life of freedom for their children and their children's children? I know instinctively that they must have hoped and dreamed—they could not have survived without hope.

And finally, *Love*. What did these bruised and exploited people know of love? They certainly knew little of neighborly love, unless it was the love they shared for one another.

I imagined a slave who worked the fields of corn and tobacco that supplied the estate's needs. How had she fared? Had her spirit been broken as well as her body? Did she lose hope that her race would ever rise up against these slavemasters?

Was she born in America, or had she been uprooted from her life in Africa? Was she pulled away from her parents, her extended family, her tribe when she was sold into slavery in a land of strange foods and bitter days? Was she ripped away from a position of respect among her villagers, among her people on the "Dark Continent"?

I wondered about the histories behind the "colored people" buried here. Perhaps one was a hunter or a village elder in his homeland. Perhaps one was a queen, or some kind of royalty in her native land. We would never know, their individual histories having been forgotten as soon as their broken bodies came to rest in the Old Dominion.

Not only will we never know of their specific stories, I thought, *but they will never know ours. They will never know that their grandchildren and great-grandchildren and great-great-grandchildren were free and a few even became prosperous in the land called America.*

As we sat there together, a steady stream of tears started rolling down my face. Charles looked concerned. The kids stared at me blankly, not understanding why their mother was crying. I surprised even myself with the intensity of emotion that swelled within me.

Taking a deep breath, I began to explain what I felt— how I hoped that somehow these forgotten slaves would know that we made it—that even though their lives were difficult and hard and rough, and painfully short, even though they were driven hard for another man's profit and glory, even though they had hopes and aspirations and dreams for their kids and their families that they never saw come true, in the end—we made it. We really did!

I tried to explain to my children that making it didn't mean that we'd arrived because we lived in a house in the suburbs and drove a station wagon with fake wood paneling on the sides. I was not referring to the Polo emblem emblazoned on my sons' shirts, nor the jobs that gave us salaries and prestige. That was not what I meant. At that moment I was thinking about the richness of who we are as a people. I was thinking of how the African-American community had survived everything that the hostile culture had thrown at us: first kidnapped, raped, beaten, enslaved, lynched, and then intimidated, exploited, and offered the false freedom of a Jim Crow existence.

In spite of all the obstacles, we survived. The tears I shed were tears of pride—pride in being part of a race that had weathered a tremendous storm, had been battered and tossed, and yet still sailed.

How I wished these earlier men and women could know of the strides our people have made. What would they think if they could come alive today and see their children's children graduating from high schools and colleges in record high numbers, becoming doctors, businessmen, teachers, politicians, day-care workers, and CEO's of companies? I imagined the pride that they would feel as I introduced them to men and women like Dr. Ben Carson, a world-renowned surgeon; General Colin Powell, Chairman of the Joint Chiefs of Staff and President Bush's top military advisor; Dr. Louis Sullivan, Secretary of Health and Human

Services, and in charge of one of the largest budgets in the world.

And I thought about what I would tell this slave if she asked, as I knew she would, how we had survived. *How had we done it? What pulled us through?*

I thought about my own life. The fifth of six children, I was born in a public-housing project to an alcoholic father and a mother on public assistance—born in an era when I couldn't ride at the front of the bus or use the public libraries. How had I been able to rise from humble beginnings to graduate from college, help run a multi-million dollar business, become a national spokesperson for the National Right to Life Committee, and eventually work in the Executive Office of the President of the United States? And I thought about how little of that climb was made possible by my natural abilities and how much came from a family, culture, and community that nurtured and strengthened me.

And I thought about African-Americans who are still in chains—the ones who are not "making it"—our people who are enslaved to alcohol, drugs, and the deception of no-commitment sex. What would this slave who used to fear violence from the slavemaster think if I took her to our urban centers to witness young black men killing other young black men? Could she even begin to understand those pariahs who become rich by peddling drugs and causing death, destruction, and violence in their own communities? She probably would not be surprised by the racism, poverty, and lack of opportunities that still exist. Could she, whose heart was broken as her family was torn apart and sold off to distant plantations, understand children growing up with only one parent because their father had willingly turned his back on his responsibilities and walked away? Volumes have been written about all these pathologies. Less has been written about those African-Americans who survived the obstacle course called America.

"The character of our people, a culture rich with strong values and a community committed to each other, has been the key to our survival," I would tell this slave in our conversation. "We made it because we maintained our faith, hope, and love, just as the monument said. We found strength in the community. Throughout our struggle, we fought to keep a sense of humor and to develop deep, resilient joy. We understood the value of equipping ourselves with the tools of knowledge. Our failures and our losses have come when we jettisoned these traditional sources of our strength."

My mind wandered as the late afternoon sun began to cast shadows on our outstretched legs. What would my slave friend tell us if she could speak to us now? I listened for whispers in the wind.

Would she shake her head in disgust at my children in their polo shirts and designer jeans? Would she reprimand us, saying, "I hope you haven't forgotten what we did. I hope you haven't forgotten how hard it was for us."

I don't think that she would begrudge my children their material possessions, their creature comforts. It would undoubtedly please her to see that there was, at least for some black children, a measure of equality, for on the outside, except for the color of their skin and the texture of their hair, my kids looked very much like their counterparts in the white family ahead of us in line. I think she would be pleased at that.

But I think that she would caution me. I think that she would plead with me to remember how we had survived. I could almost hear her tell me, *"Never forget how our people made it, never forget what brought you through."*

I thought about the one month out of the calendar year that we call Black History month, a month where someone else—usually the public schools—teaches us about the African-American experience. The schools could teach my children about George Washington Carver and Frederick Douglass and Mary McCleod Bethune. Through their storytelling hour, I could rely on the local library to bring to life Sojourner Truth and the underground railroad. Even Alex

Haley and Spike Lee would do their part by bringing Kunte Kinte and Malcolm X to the movie and television screens.

But who would tell my kids about Maggie Walker, a distant relative who shortly after the Civil War formed one of the first black-owned banks in the nation, a bank still helping minorities buy their own homes and start their own businesses today? Who would tell them about their great-grandmother, a freed slave who became a seamstress and put her children through school? Who would tell them about the freedman farmers who chided the sun for tarrying in the morning, and who tilled and harvested another man's land in the hope that their sons would one day till their own land? Who was going to tell my children about their spiritual heritage, about churches that met in basements and barns? Who would testify about the selfless giving of those first black churches? Who would hum spirituals so tender and healing that they could salve a field-weary flesh?

Who would tell them about mamas wise enough to make a king's feast from the scraps off the tables that she served? Who, if not us, would tell them about the men who took jobs as janitors and dishwashers and anything else so that they could provide for their families? Who would tell them about the black educators who valued education so much that they would sometimes risk their lives to teach young black children when it was against the law to do so? Indeed, who would tell them about the marchers and protesters who dotted our family tree, brave men and women who had fought against injustice for great-grand-children, nieces and nephews, and first-cousins that they would never know?

It was time to leave the cool sanctuary of the slave cemetery. In a hush of recognition, our children had begun to understand that they had more to thank than a mom or dad who gave them an allowance and nagged at them to do their homework. They had begun to think about where they came from and why it matters.

In the shadows of the boxwoods they saw the connection between their mom and dad and the monument to

George Washington's slaves, and they would never be the same.

Nor would Charles and I.

I made several promises that day, promises to unknown ancestors and the God that gave them strength. "Lord, help me start giving each of my children their inheritance now."

As we gathered our things to leave, I looked back at the lonely marker of the unknown slaves and made one last promise before moving on: *I will never forget where I came from. Never!*

chapter two

HUMBLE BEGINNINGS

I'VE HEARD THE STORY so many times that I can almost remember being there. My father and brothers weren't home the sultry June night that I was born. They were hunting bullfrogs in the swamp out back with flashlights and burlap sacks. Ten-year-old Ted had stuffed about as many in his sack as his daddy had. The other sons, Peter and Lucky, were still too young to be of much use, but they went along to shine the flashlight when the others went in for a catch. They would also hold the light on the critters when Daddy used the axe from the woodshed to cut off the hind quarters. The boys were looking forward to bringing them home to Mama, who would shake the frog legs in a bag with flour, salt, and pepper, and then sear them in oil.

Home was a salty stretch of land in the black section of Portsmouth, Virginia. It was a region that couldn't decide if it was country or small town. Portsmouth was cosmopolitan enough to have crabcakes on the menu at the local soul food restaurant and indoor toilets in the homes of most of the black folks.

The only black doctor in town couldn't be located to deliver me. He was a friend of the family, and I was named for his wife, Kay, but the only ones in the house with Mama when she was in labor were a neighbor and a nurse midwife who stepped in to help Mama give birth. It was the nurse who brought me into the kitchen to wash me off and then laid my crying self on the kitchen table for all the males in the family to marvel at.

And marvel they did at the little girl who had followed four boys. I would be the only one of six children to wear pink. My daddy used to like excuses to drink, so he said, "Hell, a baby girl! I'll drink to that!" And he did—for the next thirty years.

I was the third Coles baby to be born at 94 Carver Circle, a humble old house with linoleum floors and peeling, painted walls. Our neighborhood was a series of small houses that had been converted from army barracks after the war. The remodeling consisted of dividing the living space into rooms and sticking a coal-burning stove in the kitchen. It didn't take much imagination to picture our house in its glory years during the war. It had all the charm of a cement mixer.

The house was a tight fit for the Coles family. Only two bedrooms—one for my parents and me, and another for the four boys. But little boys being the way they are, my brothers were outdoors crabbing, gathering wood, or playing in the woods more often than they were inside. The only time my mother was really pressed to have a bigger home was when she was pregnant and her tiny four-foot-seven inch frame became as wide as it was tall.

The neighborhood was as cozy as the houses, with hardly room enough between them to stretch a laundry line. Mama's best friend was her next-door neighbor, a round-figured woman who probably came over for one too many cups of sugar, because she ended up marrying my father later in life.

The community was not as tightly knit as most southern towns, due no doubt to the fact that most of us were transplants. Portsmouth was filled with families who had been uprooted from their hometowns in search of work.

We, along with many other black families, migrated to the Tidewater area when word got around that there was work on the docks of Portsmouth. My father, along with most of the men in the neighborhood, worked at the navy yard as a longshoreman.

For a time, things were okay. A new naval shipyard had opened, and Daddy earned a steady paycheck from his work there. The money bought food and clothing, but it also bought liquor. And the liquor brought pain. My brothers later told me about the vicious verbal spats that my father and mother would have over his drinking.

My father was a man who wanted more than a black man in his day could have: a job utilizing his talents and skills, a paycheck big enough to feed his wife and children, respect from the white man. None of these things came easily for a black man in the segregated South of the forties and fifties. The work at the yards was good while it lasted, but it didn't last long. He took very hard his inability to provide for us and hid his failure in long sips of whiskey.

Bernard A. Coles, Sr., was the type of man who defies easy labeling: "family man," "alcoholic," "devoted husband," "aficionado of classical music," "abusive husband and father." During various periods of his life he was all of these. The range of his character was as stunning as the range of his melodic voice. I remember the gentle strokes that he saved for the face of his only daughter. And I remember, too, his drinking and how drastically his personality changed when his breath smelled of whiskey.

He was a desperation drinker who drank to numb the pain of a lifetime of frustration. He died a slow death, slowly drowning in stifled hopes and wasted talents. The one thing that every friend or foe agreed on regarding Daddy was that he was "one smart man." Even in his youth he was steps ahead of his friends. In high school he was a champion debater. As captain of Richmond's black high school's all-time best debate team, his portrait hung in the hallway of Armstrong High School for more than fifty years. His passion for argument earned him a reputation as a quick thinker and smooth talker, skills that would well serve his entrepreneurial streak.

When Daddy was still in his teens, he subcontracted out his paper route. He took on five or six routes from the *Richmond Times*, then, while pocketing the middleman's share, hired schoolmates to deliver the papers for him. His creative capitalism continued in college when he rented out a community hall, the Ten-West-Leigh, and turned it into a nightclub. He hired a band, and charged admission for the "dance." He made enough spending money from these entrepreneurial endeavors to splurge on a few dates and a lot of bottles.

I don't think that he ever quite outgrew his passion for debate. He'd argue with just about anyone about just about anything, and win. People said that he could defend an ice cube in hell. Unfortunately, there weren't many opportunities for an articulate black man in those days. He thought once about going into the ministry, not for any personal conviction about God, but to make money. He was certain that there had to be some way to cash in on his oratorical skills, but Mama, who saw right through his preaching ambitions, cut that one off quickly.

He had a brilliant mind, but school never held his interest. The opportunity cost was too high. It was not so much that he couldn't afford college as that he couldn't afford not to work. Especially not after he met and fell in love with my mother. In his mind, being a husband and bringing home the bacon were inseparable; therefore, soon after they married, he dropped out of college at Virginia Union to find work.

Breaks were few. A man with childhood dreams of being a chemist, or a doctor, found himself trapped in servile tasks. He took menial jobs, at times scrubbing the floors of the local schools that his children weren't allowed to attend, at times working as a short-order cook. For a spell he provided for his family by being a security guard. But it never lasted. Jobs came and went with the seasons so that he and my mother never felt the security of a steady, albeit low, income. God had fashioned him a man with the instinct to provide for his family, and this man knew no greater hurt than the inability to keep food on his wife's table and heat for his kids' home. My father was smart, handsome, and chronically unemployed.

He had also been blessed him with an ear for music and with a deep, lyrical voice. I can remember him walking through the house, singing from somewhere deep inside, "That old man river, he just keeps rolling, he just keeps rolling along." And then picking up one of the kids, he would growl in his stage voice, "Tote that barge! Lift that bail! You get a little drunk and you land in jail!" But his gift was also a curse. Maybe it was the incongruity between his loves in life—the arts, venture capitalism, and his daily fare. This was a man who loved opera, who sang arias in the shower, who won several amateur singing competitions, but the closest he came to using his gifts and talents was a stint as a singing waiter.

Yet even when the passage of time left him a leathery, old, shaking alcoholic, he never lost that sense of quiet nobility that set him apart. There was something you'd notice about him as he strolled past you on the street. His carriage was just a little too dignified for a man of his station. He was fun-loving, given to spontaneous eruptions of laughter. I would watch him laugh, and try to imitate the way his whole frame shook with his mirth. On more than one occasion his sense of humor saved him from a certain whopping with Mama's frying pan.

Life in Portsmouth proved a trying time for my mother. She was a simple woman, as simple as her name, Sue. In her mind there were very few things in life worth getting "fussed up about," but family was one of them. She would later say that she felt as if she had been snatched from her nest—her support system of sisters, relatives, neighbors, and church family—when she and Daddy left Richmond for Portsmouth.

The youngest of six girls of a prominent family, she was treated as the baby. She was wholly unprepared for life as a mother of six, with an alcoholic husband. And her life was tinged with a sad irony that she, the princess who grew up pampered and spoiled by the family, would one day serve as her sisters' domestic.

There must have been a lot of discussion over Sunday dinner at my Aunt Etna's up in Richmond on what to do about sister Sue whose no-good husband wasn't taking care of her or the children. Shortly after I was born, another of Mama's sisters, Pearl, and her husband, J. B., came down to Portsmouth, packed up Mama and the five children, and brought us back to Richmond. I was three months old at the time, too young to notice the "I told you so" that was in the air if not on their lips. Mama had shocked and disappointed the family when she and my father dropped out of college to marry, especially since they didn't "have to."

The move back to Richmond was intended to allow my mama's siblings to keep an eye on their youngest sister and, I suppose, to give them something to talk about among themselves. The question of where we would all live was soon solved by my father. He had two great-aunts who lived together in a rickety Victorian home on 1100 North Second Street. One of them passed away shortly after we arrived in town. Daddy's side of the family decided that it would suit everyone's needs if we moved in with great-great-aunt Duk.

Aunt Duk lived in a huge house with carved wooden lattice work and high ceilings. Its many dark, musty rooms were a playground for ghoulish fascinations, which helps explain why all the ghost stories my brothers told growing up had that eerie old house as the setting. It was so big and so scary; there were rooms my brothers didn't even go into the whole two-to-three years we lived there. One place we never wandered into was old Aunt Duk's room, a sunless back room off the second floor at the end of a long and lonesome hallway.

To this day my brothers are convinced that house was visited by haunts and ghouls who had some sort of relationship with the old matriarch of the house who (we kids suspected) was really a witch. Aunt Duk certainly looked the part. Age had taken some of her height, and what she had left bent over like a wilted violet. Her skin was shriveled and hung loose in folds from her bony frame. She had habits that scared the boys, like spending the day holed up in her room alone only to come out at night to creep down the hallways for no particular reason.

Fear made us an even closer bunch of siblings. There were no complaints when Mama instructed us to do all of our playing in the large downstairs living room during the cold winter months. It was only at night that we'd venture upstairs to slip into our beds, whose sheets Mama had warmed with an iron. The fire that Peter and Ted would stoke sputtered out some time near midnight, and the winter chill would seep into our floors and bedposts.

"Goodnight, sleep tight, don't let Jack Frost get you tonight," Mama would say as she tucked us into bed. And we would pull the warm sheet up to our chin and try not to move all night lest some of the cold air find its way down to our toes. During Christmas season and the frosty months following, we could see our breath as we whispered goodnights into the bedroom air. During that season Mama would pile coats, clothes, and old towels on top of us to help keep us warm as we lay in bed. None of us minded being doubled and tripled up in bed then. The more bodies the warmer—and the better.

That house also had the luxury of indoor plumbing. We were proud as peacocks that ours was the only backyard on the street with no outhouse. For a while we even took our baths in the large porcelain tub in the upstairs bathroom. But practicality won out over indulgence during the winter months. A dripping, naked streak across the tiled floor of that unheated room was enough to send shivers up your spine even after the iron-warmed bed enveloped you in its warmth.

The older boys had chores around the house, which they would dutifully perform while we younger ones followed at a respectful distance and observed. I especially remember Ted's jobs of feeding the pet chickens he kept on the second-floor balcony and keeping the fire lit in the coal furnace. This lighting of the furnace was one of the more interesting chores to observe, and my younger brother, Arthur, and I tagged along whenever we could.

One morning as we toddled around after Ted, Arthur opened up the furnace as he had just seen his older brother do, and he stuck his face in the opening. The next second the whole house echoed with the blast of the furnace exploding. "Jesus Christ!" Ted roared in a burst almost as loud as the explosion as he pulled his soot-faced little brother away from the furnace. Arthur had burned his eyebrows right off his face. We knew that someone was going to get it, not because we had let Arthur burn himself but because someone had used the Lord's name in vain.

Mama, who called out to God routinely through her exclamations, had absolutely no tolerance for those who called upon the Lord in a disrespectful manner. As my brothers got older, if a "damn" or a "hell" slipped out after spending a little too much time with their father, they could expect a quick reprimand. But if you ever took the Lord's name in vain, you'd better duck! Maybe that's why, to this day, I cannot bear to hear the name of the Lord used in any manner other than reverently. It really irritates me, but in all honesty, I guess I'm a little gun-shy—I half expect the offender to be struck down. I remember being on a crowded elevator once when someone whispered an angry "Jeeezus Cha-rist!" I found myself subconsciously looking around the elevator for Mama's size-5 shoe coming at him at high velocity.

Like all mothers, Mama had words to live by. These sayings formed the staple of her conversation and hinted at the homegrown faith in Jesus that was as much a part of her as her broad smile and smoky brown skin. "Lord, have mercy!" was her response to just about anything alarming or interesting. "Mama, ain't no more flour in the bin," one of us would say. "Lord, have mercy!" she'd say. Another child would say, "Mama, I got an A on my spelling test." "Lord, have mercy!" Mama would answer with a smile lighting her angelic face.

Family rituals provided a comforting reliability during those chaotic days. I knew that I could count on greens at Sunday dinner, baths on Saturday night, and Mama's always taking the six of us to church on Sundays (my little brother, Tony, was born after the family returned to Richmond). Baths were taken in a round tub in the kitchen. Each child had his turn and then Tony and I would get in together. Each night before bed, Mama required us to get on our knees to say our prayers. This latter routine became a bit burdensome during cold spells when the cold of winter seeped through the wooden floor. Once when Lucky dared to complain about this ritual, Mama quickly cut him off: "Son, you get on your feet to play football, you crouch in the bushes to play tag, you can sure enough get on your knees to pray to your God!" That was the last time any of us complained about kneeling for prayer.

Life on Second Street was marked by a fear and insecurity that had less to do with the ghouls we imagined than with the fights we witnessed between our parents. There was a battle warring in Daddy's soul between his love for his family and his craving for drink. "You better stop with that whiskey," Mama would say with tired hope, "it's going to kill you someday!" But Daddy would brush off her concern: "I know it, but I'm gonna drink it till the day I die."

Their words were prophetic.

It wasn't three months later that Daddy took a mysterious fall off the second-story balcony. We all heard the thump his body made when it hit the ground two flights down. A couple of men from the neighborhood brought his bleeding body into the house, and some of the women put a sheet on the sofa in the living room and told the men to lay him there. In the blur of frightened activity, someone set Tony and me in a chair beside him, and we watched, horrified and fascinated, as his blood dripped down the sofa into pools on the rug.

As it turned out, alcohol almost killed my father that

day, but it also saved him. His body was so relaxed when he hit the ground that he came away from the fall with a sprained back, a few broken bones, but no major damage.

He left the hospital in a cast from his hips to his neck to immobilize his sprained back. He also had two additional body parts casted, his left leg and his right arm. Three weeks hadn't passed when he told Mama, "Get a knife and cut this damn thing off. I'm itching!" But believing in the doctors who had said that he needed at least six weeks in that cast, she wouldn't do it. So Daddy went and filled the bathtub full of water and sat in it till all three of his casts were a gooey plaster mess. And then he pulled them off, one by one.

Daddy's body healed a lot faster after that incident than Mama's broken heart. His physical fall off the balcony corresponded with a spiritual fall that he had taken in his life. Mama was always pleading with him to stop drinking, but he had chosen his first love: whiskey. Daddy was sliding down a greased pole to self-destruction.

His jobs became even more sporadic and short-lived. He "aced" the test to become a letter carrier with the post office, no small feat without the added points of military service, but he was as unreliable as he was smart, and that job soon went the way of many others.

The job we kids all loved was when he worked in the toy section of Thalhimer's, Richmond's largest department store. The area beneath our Christmas tree was usually a pretty sparse scene, but the year that Daddy worked for the department store, we had every kind of toy you could think of and even some we had never thought of. Daddy would rescue all the broken or chipped toys from the dumpster and bring them home to fix up and put under our tree. How we wished Daddy could have kept that job, but it went the way of all the others as Daddy's drinking continued.

● ● ●

These are not pleasant memories, but they are ones I will never forget. I am not ashamed of my early years; of my abusive, alcoholic father. Like it or not, he was my daddy. From him I inherited a gift for debate that helped me take the heat that came with being national spokesperson for the National Right to Life Committee. From him I also gained an appreciation for the arts. And from him I began to understand the chains of addiction that still enslave many of us. Daddy wanted only to be able to provide for the family he loved. When that couldn't happen, he hid his frustration in a bottle.

For every black man drinking on the street corners I pass on the way to work in the morning, I can never forget what it was like to see my daddy drunk. And for every mama cleaning hotel rooms to help send her children to college, I can never forget my mama's quiet dignity in the face of sadness. It is both *because* of them and *for* them that I have strived to make something of my life.

Isn't that what both of them really wanted? Isn't that what the mamas and daddies arriving from Africa would have wished could happen some day?

• • •

Fighting words began to take the place of conversation between my parents, and Daddy's threats of violence turned into slaps and punches. We younger children were shielded from his brutality, but Mama and the older boys bore on their bodies the heaviness of his rage. The tension between my parents and the constant grind of poverty was hardest on Ted, the oldest child, and the one who stood in for Daddy when he couldn't perform his duties as head of the household.

An idea began to germinate in Ted's mind that if only Mama and the kids could get away from Daddy, then everything would be all right. Who knows how long he had mulled over that thought in his mind before he set about on a plan of action? One morning when most of the kids were out playing and Aunt Duk was visiting a friend, Ted and Mama were alone in the kitchen. As soon as she went into the living room to do her mending, he stole up the steps to one of the bedrooms. There in the secrecy of the dark, he set a mattress on fire and slipped back downstairs.

Smoke began to filter down the steps as he played with Arthur and me under Mama's watchful eyes, but no one noticed the gray cloud descending the stairs. Ted was bouncing me on his knees and his nervousness made for an especially bumpy ride, but still no one but Ted noticed the acrid smell. When he saw the flames starting to lick the banister and that still no one had noticed, he finally yelled, "Mama, the house is on fire!" and the four of us ran out the back door. Firemen were soon on the scene.

Then Ted suddenly remembered his chickens on the second-story balcony. He was off like a cat, running straight for the burning house. A fireman grabbed his arm and tried to hold him back, but he wiggled out of the man's grip and ran into the house. We were all very relieved to see him emerge from the back door a few moments later, with three soot-blackened chickens flapping in his arms.

Ted hadn't succeeded in burning down the house. For all the excitement the mysterious fire had generated in the neighborhood, the flames had only damaged a few rooms and a mattress—but his underlying purpose, to free Mama and the kids from his sometimes violently abusive father, was achieved. It was only a few short months after the fire that Mama left Daddy for good and moved us into a public-housing project called Creighton Court.

chapter three
CREIGHTON COURT

I WAS PROUD TO BE one of the Creighton Court girls. Our colors were red and white: red for Kool-Aid tongues and white for chalk-dusted palms that had drawn scores of hopscotch squares on the blacktop. We also filled the sidewalks with pictures of cats and frogs and smiling faces, but our masterpieces never lasted long because the boys in the neighborhood ignored our protests and walked over them, smudging the figures into white clouds.

Because we lived in federally subsidized housing, we were called "project" kids—the bottom of the pecking order in Richmond. Even the black kids who lived up on the "hill"–the more affluent black neighborhood–called us "project niggers." Consequently, we knew no sweeter thrill than beating one of the hill kids at double-dutch, kickball, baseball, tag, football, or any of the multitude of games that we played in the open field between our neighborhoods. The older you were, the more serious the rivalry. Football games between the hill kids and the Creighton Court boys were the centerpiece of our competitions. Both sides would spend weeks practicing in the hot afternoon sun, devising elaborate plays for the big game. On the day of the match, the hill team, which was made up almost entirely of one group of kin, would show up with professional shoulder pads, cloth helmets, and cleats. Our team was doing well if everyone showed up with shoes. My brothers would stuff socks into their pants to make thigh and knee pads. On the way to the game, they would wad up old T-shirts and stuff them under their shirts on top of their shoulders. The idea was to fashion padding to help soften the hits they would take, but I think that they also did it to make them look bigger and more intimidating.

They took their share of hits. I don't think that my brothers ever understood why God blessed the hill kids doubly: Not only did they come from families with money, but they were incredible athletes as well.

Our rivalry with the well-to-do hill kids instilled in my brothers and me an us-against-them mentality and defined our mission in life to prove that we were just as smart, just as fast, just as good as they were. This drive to excel was sharpened by an acute awareness of being the black sheep of our extended family.

In those days, you weren't known simply as "Tom," "Colby," or "Ann." Your name might be "Eva," but you were known as "Eva, Pastor Lewis's daughter." Or you were "Larry, of the North Carolina Washingtons." An introduction wasn't complete if the name of at least one relative wasn't tagged on, or at least some fact about the family was included. These name tags provided a comforting context, a way to allow strangers to place you in their world. You were connected.

Thus, it wasn't unusual that I would go over to a new friend's house to play and a mother would ask me whose little girl I was. I learned to respond that I was Kay Coles and that my mama was Sue-of-the-Armistead-sisters.

Most of the time these addendums to your name weren't neutral. They usually transcribed a certain bit of information, or notoriety, about your origins. If you were fortunate, this appellation conveyed a positive family association. In that sense, we were lucky, because my mother was one of the Armistead sisters. Our name carried currency. In those days it meant something to be a Foster, or a Brown, or an Armistead. Our family was among a handful of well-respected families in Richmond.

The Armistead sisters earned their good name by going to college, holding interesting jobs, and marrying well. All professionals, they were black middle class before we even knew there was such a thing. As the saying went, "They had done good."

All, that is, except Mama. The youngest of five sisters, she was treated as the baby, pampered, and protected. Perhaps that's why she so easily fell for my handsome, charming, and chronically jobless father.

The adults who were aware of our situation, and in my childhood universe that included just about every adult I knew, were fairly adept at hiding their condescension or their pity. Children, however, are painfully candid and can be amazingly cruel. Through subtle (and not-so-subtle) ways, I was constantly reminded that I was poor—that we were the black sheep of an otherwise decent family.

From the beginning, then, I had something to prove. Faced with the choice of believing their harsh words or rejecting their judgment, I fought to prove them wrong. I fought back with grades, achievement, and clean living. Decades later I still have to wonder if some of my drive is not still directed at proving "them" wrong.

What we lacked in prestige, my brothers and I made up for in cohesiveness. I took great comfort in the security of having five brothers who, I knew, would beat the spit out of anyone who dared hurt me. Everyone in the neighborhood knew that to mess with one of us meant that there were five other Coles siblings that they were going to have to answer to as well. This reputation earned us the nickname "Sue Nation," a tribute to our mama and the protective loyalty of our family.

The move from Second Street and a two-parent family to Creighton Court and a fatherless family in public housing served to strengthen our tribal mentality. Before the move, we were all very curious about this strange thing known as public housing. My first impression of the "projects," as we called them, was of rather pleasant looking buildings surrounded by grass and playgrounds.

I'll never forget how proud Mama was as we drove along Nine-Mile Road and she saw our new home for the first time. "That's my little place right there," she gushed. Once inside however, it lost all of its humanity. In each of the five rooms of our townhouse apartment, rough gray cinder block walls met an equally dreary concrete floor. The worst adjustment was to our new roommates: hundreds and hundreds of cockroaches! They would crawl up the drain in the bathtub and find their way into virtually every nook and cranny in the apartment.

One advantage of having five brothers was that Mom and I could call on them to come kill the roaches that we spotted on the table, or in the silverware drawer. Even today, I call my husband or one of my sons to squash an insect for me. (Old habits die hard.) Often as I lay in bed at night, I would fight sleep, worrying that one of the brown creepers would fall from the ceiling and crawl around on my face as I slept. Each night there was a ritual that I would perform religiously—a ritual that lent a certain sense of comfort and security. After brushing my teeth, I would get on my knees and say my prayers out loud for Mama to hear. After pulling back the sheets to check for any wayward bugs, I'd sing songs to myself to take my mind off the roaches that came out when the light went off. Each morning I would check my shoes before putting them on, to make sure that none had taken up residence in them the night before.

"The insect problem," as Mama referred to our roaches, was accepted as part of life in a public-housing complex. The communal nature of the projects meant that no matter how clean you kept your individual unit, just one dirty or careless family in the building could harbor an entire population of roaches.

We fought a constant battle to push them back—not to

let them overtake our home—but no barrier could resist them. It seemed useless to try to kill them off one by one. For every one that we captured, there was another behind him eager to take his place.

Winter nights were spent doubled and tripled up in bed. Because I was the smallest, I usually ended up in a bed with at least two brothers. I loved to press my cold nose against their warm necks and giggle as they yipped and shivered. I felt safe, and warm, and loved. As we huddled in bed together, I thought of all the poor boys and girls who didn't have brothers or sisters they could snuggle with in bed. "Lord, bless the children who don't have anyone to sleep with to keep them warm at night," I'd whisper on my way toward sleep.

I consider myself fortunate that we never had to endure the public housing that came later. Over a period of time, public housing seemed to be designed to cram as many people as possible into as tight a space as possible, generating the high-rise tenements where more often than not you'll find poor people being warehoused. When I tour housing projects today, I'm shocked at the trash-strewn, bullet-scarred streets ruled by fatherless teenage boys. Some of the worst inner-city projects are zones of lawlessness where law-abiding citizens are virtually held captive in their own homes.

Though Creighton Court certainly had its unsavory element, we lived under too many strictly enforced regulations to ever succumb to lawlessness. Some of these rules proved beneficial. For example, residents were required to keep the outdoor appearance of their public housing unit in top condition. To ensure that residents didn't allow their homes to become run-down and neglected looking, a fifty-cent fine was charged for any piece of trash found in your yard. My younger brother, Tony, was responsible for checking our yard every day on the way to school. We were also not allowed to wear out the grass on our front lawns. We had an area out back where we were allowed to play sandlot football and other games that tore up the grass, but not in front.

Other regulations were downright intrusive and annoying. Tenants couldn't make improvements to their home by planting flowers, painting the walls, or putting in air conditioning. It seemed as if we were being constantly reminded by the housing authority that we were not the owners, or even real renters, but that we were wards of the housing authority. And you will never come across a more inefficient or stingy landlord than the government. In our public-housing complex on October 15 the heat came on— no matter that the trees were already bent with the weight of frost or that we were enjoying a balmy and bright Indian summer. On October 15 the heat went on and went off April 15. In the in-between months we bundled ourselves with coats and blankets to keep out the drafts. The cinder-block walls were like ice to the touch, and the floors sent shivers through socked feet.

In those days, violence was rare but not unheard of. One night my older brothers and I were walking to the store along the path between the housing units, when the night air exploded with a sound like a firecracker. A bullet slammed into the sidewalk right in front of us. The fact that the fellows shooting weren't aiming at us wasn't much of a consolation.

That kind of shooting was the exception. Teenagers didn't rule the streets as they do now. Oh, we had our share of crap games going on and even some drug sales and turf wars, but overall, adults were in control of the neighborhood. They set the tone. It wasn't any set of external rules or regulations that upheld the standards of the neighborhood but a strong sense of community and shared values that bound us together.

I will never forget coming home from the grocery store with my mother. Some women were scared to walk through that housing project at night, but Mama knew that she'd be safe. She was known for her kind spirit, and you'd think that would make her a vulnerable target, but that spirit and the respect that she gave to others made her respected by even the hustlers in the neighborhood. She would always greet them with a "Hello, Mr. So-and-so," and these same hustlers would stop shooting craps and jump up off their knees. And when Mama came through with the groceries, they'd offer to carry her bags home for her. I remember that whenever she would venture across town she would never have to stand on the bus. Someone would invariably say, "Hey; that's Mrs. Coles," and a seat would open for us.

It is a testimony to the strength of her character and her will that she raised the six of us without her man to help her with the discipline. One time Peter dared to talk back to Mama. He whispered something under his breath that we couldn't hear but knew was disrespectful. Now Mama was only four-foot-seven, and she had a difficult time smacking the boys once they crossed the six-foot mark. But on this occasion, Mama pushed Lucky's box of marbles right off the edge of the counter. Marbles spun across the floor and she nodded in Peter's direction: "Boy, pick those marbles up." As he bent over to pick them up, Mama bopped him upside the head. It didn't hurt him. In fact, he was sort of amused by Mama's cunning strategy . . . but you better believe that he got the message.

And we knew better than to disrespect any of the other adults in the community either. If Mr. Lincoln next door said, "Son, I don't think that's something your mama would want you to be doing," you knew that you'd best not do it.

The neighborhood was filled with surrogate parents like Aunt Nervy. That woman whipped us more often than our own mother did. I never have quite figured out who she was. I don't think she was even a relative, but she was nevertheless part of the enveloping set of family and friends who formed our community. She'd never threaten us with "I'll tell your mama!"—she took care of business right there on the spot. And you sure enough weren't going to go home talking about, "Mamma, Aunt Nervy hit me!" 'cause you knew that Mama would flare her nostrils and say, "For what?" And bop, you'd get it again.

Now before you make a case against this kind of discipline, let me make a distinction about the "thumpings" we got and today's tragedy of child abuse. We knew that our mother cared for us, just as we knew that the other adults who took the time to correct us wanted us to grow up and make something of our lives. Their physical "incentives" to better behavior were clear evidence of their care along with the other loving things that they did for us.

In fact, these extra sets of parents and kin in the neighborhood could be a real asset. If it weren't for Mrs. Gladys next door, I'd have gone through my entire childhood with my hair in a ponytail. With five boys, Mama wasn't much on doing hair, so she used to take me over to Mrs. Gladys, who knew how to do all sorts of fun things like feminine braids and twists.

We may have been poor, but we were a community. We did things together. Every Saturday evening, seven or eight women from the neighborhood would get together and walk twenty-five blocks to the old market on Eighteenth and Main. The market would reduce the price of all the meat on Saturday night because it would be closed on Sunday and Monday, so most of the women would make the trek together and load up on cheap meat. There was a side benefit as well: Most nights they came back with more juicy gossip than meat.

Even in the midst of my father's struggling with alcoholism and my mother's being nearly overwhelmed with the task of providing for six children, our world was calm and serene. I enjoyed the chaotic hustle-bustle of children running through the house and was never bored because I always had a playmate at hand. Even though my father was gone more than he was home, I never really felt a void, because in my world there were so many others loving me and providing care. Creighton Court had several families with neglected kids—children who didn't have anyone who thought that they were special. I knew that I was someone special because I always had my hair done nicely. Why would Mrs. Gladys waste her time doing someone's hair if that person was poor and worthless? I may have been hungry and poor, but I was *neat* and *clean* hungry and poor.

People go to great lengths today to try to re-create that sense of belonging and joyful camaraderie we had in that overstuffed house. Isn't that really the void being filled by today's urban gangs? Without the cohesive family and neighborhoods my generation knew as children, kids in our cities will find something else to belong to.

Periodically, something that seemed especially evil would invade the relative security of our neighborhood. It came hidden behind white hoods and was known by its frightening initials: KKK. They held their cross burnings in the field that we sometimes used for football games, not half a mile down the street next to the police station. The word would go through the neighborhood when the Klan was rallying, and we knew to stay indoors. It used to scare me to death when cars filled with yoo-hooing hooded whites drove down Nine-Mile Road, headed for the big rally. It never was clear in my mind that they hated us because we were black. I didn't understand racism. I just knew that they were evil people who would hurt a little girl if she was caught alone near the field on a rally night. One time Ted didn't get the word, and he went out to pick blackberries in the woods by the field. He had to hide in a bush when two hooded figures with shotguns walked right by him.

Mama and the other parents in Creighton Court had strict rules about where we children were allowed to play. The neighborhood pack would spend the early part of the day in the common play area behind the project, where someone's relative could be counted on to keep an eye on us. As the afternoon sun began to set we moved to the front, where rows of lemonade-sipping parents, grandparents, uncles, aunts, and anyone else who had a mind to remind you of your limits, minded the children.

Our boundaries were strictly marked off. We were not allowed to play outside the immediate neighborhood. Never was I to cross Nine-Mile Road, the busy two-lane street that passed in front of our building and intersected Bunche Place.

Because the other side of Nine-Mile Road was off-limits, the grass there was a vibrant green that took on its own light when the sun danced upon it. Unlike the stamped-down, limp, yellow grass that spotted the dirt in the play area out back, this grass was tall and willowy and left paths of darker green when the wind swept by.

One day after inspecting our sorry patch of dirt out back, Tony and I decided that it would be much more fun to play across the street. I would never break one of Mama's rules, at least not deliberately. She had raised me too well for that. But an idea popped into my head that seemed the perfect plan. If you followed Bunche Place long enough down the block, it ended in a cul-de-sac. Therefore, I reasoned, one could follow along the edge of the road, curve along the cul-de-sac and be safely on the other side. I grabbed Tony's hand, and we skipped the course that I had laid out in my mind and ended up on the other side of the great divide directly opposite our house. We flopped on our backs and began wiggling our arms and legs to make angels in the grass.

The sound of a slamming screen door across the street brought us to our senses. It was Mama, and she was headed straight for us with a full head of steam. She strode toward us, hitching up her dress midstep with one hand, pumping the air with the other to pick up speed.

"Lord, have mercy!" I mumbled with my heart in my throat, and I began to cry in anticipation of the spanking that her eyes told me I was soon to receive. We were barely on our feet before Mama nabbed us and began yanking us toward home.

"How many times have I told you not to cross Nine-Mile Road?" she asked, not waiting for an answer. The more Tony and I tried to explain that we hadn't really crossed the street, the angrier she got.

"I didn't raise my children to lie," she shot back and without stopping her march to the house she began whipping both of us with powerful underhand strokes on our bottoms. All three of us were crying by this point, and tears streamed down our faces. When she finally got us inside, she finished the spanking that had started in the middle of busy, two-lane Nine-Mile Road.

After the tears subsided and Mama had settled down, we finally were able to explain how we got across the street without really *crossing* the street. Then Mama got so upset for spanking us that *she* began crying. She called us, and pretty soon we were all hugging each other as Tony patted her on the back and told her that it was all right.

Even in the midst of the hollering and spankings, I knew that my mama loved me and was trying to protect us. I knew that she tried to keep us from crossing those sacred limits for our own good: to save us from getting hurt.

The love of my mother, my older brothers, and neighbors, wrapped me in a protective covering like a homemade quilt. Their love insulated me from the brutal reality of our family's circumstances, but at times, that same protective quilt covered my eyes as well as my heart, leaving me blind and therefore vulnerable to some of the dangers of my world.

Even my father, with all his problems, showered me with a gentle and profound love that became one of the layers of care that shielded me from the hurtful aspects of life in the projects. When I read about people blaming their present situation on a troubled parent, I wonder if they have forgotten even those few times when the love of a parent shines through. I prefer never to forget the good times.

For example, each time Daddy came into our apartment, he would call out my name. Hearing his deep baritone voice rolling above the other noises of the apartment, I would race from wherever I was to greet him. Every time, we played the same game. He'd bend over to look at me—brown eye to brown eye, while one hand hung behind his back.

"How much do I love you?" he'd ask.

"One hundred times," I'd shoot back coyly.

"Not enough," he'd say with a hint of disappointment in his voice.

"A thousand times," I'd tease a little more.

"Not enough." And we'd continue until I was up to a zillion, billion, trillion, cotillion, and then he'd smile and show that broad trademark smile of his and say, "That's the right answer!" And I would get the candy bar.

I never tired of this game, no matter how many times the scene would be replayed. In his eyes I could do no wrong, and vice versa. I was a special child, his only daughter.

Sometimes, how we choose to remember the circumstances of our past determines the way we decide to live out the present. When it comes to my father, a man who had more than his share of faults, I will never forget.

Daddy loved me.

chapter four
PROJECT NIGGERS

WE OFTEN HEARD LECTURES on the value of hard work, the importance of education, and such. Of course none of these sermons, though they certainly had their place, was as effective as the living example of my mother. We watched her board a bus in the cold morning hours and return after sunset, tired but ready to cook and clean for her own family. Her daily routine taught us the dignity of honest work and the incomparable satisfaction of earning a living.

When we were tempted to turn to unChristian activities to sweeten the dullness of a no-frills life, Mama always reminded us that we were better than that. How many times did we hear that the Coles family did not beg, cheat, or steal? If we were dying to have something that was the rage among the other kids, no amount of whining to Mama would get it. If we wanted it, she would tell us, "Go out and get a job to pay for it."

These principles of living applied even when our sparse diet of chicken and biscuits was cut back to biscuits and 'fat back'. A standard dinner was Hungarian goulash—Mama's name for hamburger meat with canned spaghetti and any leftovers in the refrigerator. We ate kidneys and rice when we were lucky. It used to kill us on Sunday afternoons to walk home for dinner across the neighborhood and smell fried chicken wafting through the air. That smell almost got my brother killed . . . by Mama.

Some of Ted's friends figured out that the kitchen at the elementary school could be broken into fairly easily since it had only a single lock. Now Ted was a tagalong and, true to form, he went along with them when they broke into the school's walk-in refrigerator and stole some of the plucked chickens hanging there for school lunches.

You can imagine our joy (and surprise) to see Ted come in the back door with his hands full of chickens. We started jumping up and down and doing something like a square dance right there in the kitchen. None of us asked him where he got them, knowing somewhere in the back of our minds that it'd be best not to. But there was no sense in trying to fool Mama once she got home. She had that sixth sense that mothers have that tells them exactly what their children have been up to no matter what story they come up with. She knew that Ted hadn't bought the chickens, but she waited to hear his story.

He just flat out told her he had taken them from the school, banking on the fact that she would see it as he did: not really stealing, since the school seemed such an impersonal storehouse. Stealing from the school was not like slipping into the back of Ike's Grill and making off with some of his spiced shrimp—now that was stealing! Taking things from the school was somehow different in our minds but not in Mama's.

She took those chickens by the feet and started pummeling Ted, who was ducking left and right, trying to avoid getting poked with a wing or a bill. She backed him into a corner and, with one hand still holding the birds and the other pointed right in his face, she spoke in a voice so low and forceful that you'd have thought that God was speaking: "Boy! I will *starve* before I let one of my children bring stolen food into this house."

That was all she said before she turned and opened the back door. We all watched bug-eyed as she flung those chickens into the backyard.

My brothers and I remembered that incident whenever anyone from another part of town called us "project niggers." Because of Mama's high standards, we knew who we were. We might have grown up in a public housing project, but Mama *raised* us at home. A lot of struggling single-parents and courageous grandparents know what I mean when I say that the circumstances a child grows up in are far less important than the character of the person who raises them.

We tease each other a lot about the chicken story, but the part about Mama's throwing them out the back door is always told with a certain bit of pride because the other mothers accepted the stolen chickens and cooked them that night for dinner. Our mama didn't. One simple incident taught us so much about honesty and integrity. The other boys learned that if their mothers would accept stolen chickens, then they would probably take drug money as well. The early lessons that those boys missed cost many of them their freedom and some their lives.

Mama's teaching about honesty and hard work helped define us as individuals. We knew who we were. It was also about this time that I developed a sense of pride in my people. Although I felt absolutely no emotional or spiritual ties to the land of my heritage—Africa—I had an enormous sense of respect and affection for the black community in Richmond. The Richmond of my childhood, like many other Southern towns in the 1950s, was so utterly segregated that it could more aptly be described as two Richmonds. Church Hill, the largest black neighborhood, was a city within a city. I went for months at a time without encountering even one white person. In fact, I am sure that I never had a conversation with a white person until I reached junior high school. The abundance of black-owned-and-operated businesses meant that the black community could be almost entirely self-contained and self-sufficient.

I loved to tag along with Mama and her sisters when she ran errands. I watched out the bus window as the scenery changed. As we wandered among the shops, I enjoyed the sharp smell of lake trout frying. On special occasions we even sampled some at Ike's.

We went to Second Street for ribs and to Abe's for club sandwiches. At that time, Douglas Wilder's law office (he later became the governor of Virginia) was right behind Ike's. We all guessed that he located there because of the great seafood. We even had our own drug stores and gas stations. It had to be that way because we couldn't go anywhere else. Slaughter's Hotel was where black out-of-towners stayed, and local folks went there for soul food. We had our prescriptions filled at Williams' Drug Store, and we bought our insurance from North Carolina Mutual or Universal Life.

Black folks banked at Consolidated Bank, and when I say "banked," I don't just mean that we put our money in for safekeeping. We received business and mortgage loans in return. It's a source of pride in Richmond's black community that Consolidated remained solvent during this nation's recent banking crisis. We kept our money in our community for just about everything but taxes.

Richmond, the former capital of the Confederacy, was larger and more industrialized than many of its Dixie counterparts. It was also unique in that it had a sizable population of middle-class blacks. They were mostly preachers, school teachers, dentists, doctors, or professionals, who owned and operated the black insurance companies, drugs stores, florist shops, and businesses in the black sections of town. Many of my relatives were part of this emerging black bourgeoisie.

Church Hill was the biggest black neighborhood but not the only black section of town. Virtually every quadrant of Richmond had a section within it where the black folks lived. Unlike the urban ghettos of today populated by those whom sociologists have termed the "underclass," these black neighborhoods were vertically integrated. By this I mean that lawyers lived on the same street with janitors, and housing projects like mine were situated right next to more affluent homes. We can't claim any false solidarity, though. Our choices were limited. Even those who could afford to build homes could not live in the white sections of town. This circumscribing of the black community gave rise to mixed neighborhoods where clusters of newly built and impressive homes of the black bourgeoisie were built in the midst of working class and poor neighborhoods.

The almost complete separation of the races left both sides to conjure up opinions of each other from secondhand stories and impersonal contacts. Enduring myths grew in the cracks of knowledge left by segregation. One such myth is that black men don't want to work. Another is that black folks are inherently stupid and lazy. But stereotypes went both ways. You would have had a hard time convincing me that white people were anything but cold, uptight, and rude. Segregation was a dark, impenetrable chasm and provided fertile ground for the growth of all sorts of misunderstandings and barbarous acts. Like the time the Klan burned a cross on my Uncle Oliver's front lawn.

The whole family was proud of Uncle Oliver. He and Thurgood Marshall graduated together from Howard University. They were number one and number two in their class. Oliver Hill was really one of our cousins, but he was so much older we called him "uncle" out of respect. While growing up, we didn't understand much of what he did although we knew that it had something to do with helping black people and that he was a hero not only in our family but to black people across America. Uncle Oliver wasn't physically imposing, but he had such an aura of strength about him that you knew immediately that he wasn't a man to be messed with. He was a good-looking man, and his deep, bronze complexion nearly matched the leather brief-case case that was his constant companion. His habit of fixing a steady gaze on whomever he was talking to let you know he wasn't much on chitchat. He had the look of a man who had seen too much of war. When the Klan burned a

cross in his yard, he kept it and hung it up in his garage like
a trophy, or a challenge.

The racism and rejection by the white community was,
no doubt, partly responsible for the strong bonds within the
black community. The walls of racial prejudice encouraged a
sense of shared experience and suffering among blacks who
may have had little else in common besides their blackness.
This explains in part why then, and even today, a black
doctor is likely to feel more comfortable with a black auto
mechanic than with his fellow white physicians. It is a sad
commentary on the state of the church in America that
blacks are more likely to call one another "sister" and
"brother" than are Christians apt to use these terms.

Segregation also gave rise to unimaginable acts of
solidarity and kindness within the black community. When
you couldn't make your rent because you had lost your job
or had a medical emergency, you threw a "rent party."
Word would get around that you had lost your job and that
you were having a rent party. Friday night you'd cook a
bunch of food and have some drinks on hand to sell;
everyone would come to your place and sit around and talk,
and by the end of two days you'd have enough money to
pay your rent. These parties were benefit dinners without a
planning committee. We survived because we depended on
one another. Today that same person may go jump off a
bridge because he can't figure out how he's going to get by
his financial crisis.

We also got along because we helped each other. We
found ways to be very creative. For example, we weren't
allowed to swim in any of the city pools in Richmond, but
that didn't mean we didn't swim. There was one pool in
Richmond where black kids could swim. It was called
"Brook Pool" and was run by Arthur Ashe's father. But we
did most of our swimming in creeks and at "Pretty Blue," a
big gravel pit that was as deep as it was wide. The boys
would head over there after a hot, dusty day of caddying.
Everyone had to put up the money that he or she had
earned that day. And if they were too afraid to dive in, they

would lose their money. We were creative when it came to fun.

I don't ever want to forget being called a "project nigger." Those words stung—they still do, but they also remind me of the times in which Mama taught us what we were made of. They remind me of my friends living in segregated Richmond and how we all made the best of our lives despite not having privileges that the white kids had. As I look at the scores of young black kids in the city living "down" to the expectations forced on them by an uncaring community, how I wish that they could develop a higher vision for who they are. These are precious children in God's sight. We must never forget that.

chapter five
LIVING WITH PEARL

T H A T   I   W A S my Aunt Pearl and Uncle J. B.'s favorite, attracting more than my share of hugs and presents, didn't surprise me. After all, as the only daughter among five boys I was often the center of attention.

Had I been a bit older, however, I might have noted a wistful look of envy in Aunt Pearl's countenance when her eyes fell upon Mama and me talking or playing together. Perhaps I might have noticed how often her eyes were focused on me during our visits, following my every move as I skipped about the house. Perhaps, too, I might have wondered at the predictable routine that we followed every time I'd go there for the weekend. First, my hair would be rebraided and then Aunt Pearl would tell me to go put on a more appropriate dress, which I came to understand meant one of the made-to-wear dresses that she had bought for me at a store. I was only five at the time, and her doting attention made me believe that perhaps fairy godmothers really do exist and that she was mine.

Pearl and J. B. began bringing me out to their home more and more. Often I would stay overnight and eventually every weekend. I looked forward to these times of respite away from all the noise and confusion of our apartment. As we'd pull away from Creighton Court in my uncle's Chrysler Imperial, I would prop myself up on my knobby knees to watch the cinder-gray building melt into the oil-stained Nine-Mile Road. Once Creighton Court was out of sight, I'd turn my body and attention to focus on the neat rows of houses we passed on the right and left.

During the car ride out to their home, my stomach was often knotted up inside with excitement and anticipation. Aunt Pearl and Uncle J. B. always managed to pick up some sort of present for me when I came for the weekend. When they gave me their gifts, I didn't have to guess how much they loved me as I did to get my father's candy bar. Leading me inside, Aunt Pearl would casually say, "Oh, Kay, I think there's something for you on your bed."

On these visits I truly felt like a princess. Not only did I have my own room, I had my very own bed! It was the first time that I had ever slept in a bed without at least two of my brothers, let alone all by myself. My room also contained a small dresser that became stuffed with the play clothes, church dresses, and purses that they had given me as presents in the past. *How had I gotten so lucky?* I wondered, and I made a pledge to thank God every night for his goodness to me.

Then one afternoon Mama called me into the kitchen and gave me the news. As she set me up on her lap, close to her bosom as she did on the few occasions when she tried to do my hair, I knew that something was wrong. Her tear-swollen eyes confirmed my hunches.

"Child, opportunity don't come knocking but so many times in a person's life . . . You know that, don't you, Kay?'

"Yes, ma'am," I murmured.

"Well," she continued, "your Aunt Pearl and Uncle J.B., because they love you so much and want to provide opportunities for you. . . ."

Pause.

"They want you to go and live with them."

There it was. The dagger had struck, and I felt my heart

bleeding inside of me. Words would not come out—only tears and a muffled moan.

"Now Kay, Pearl and J. B. can give you things that your mama could never give you. You'll be able to go on vacations. You'll be able to have nice clothes, even go to college one day." With every item that she added to the list, I shook my head in rejection.

"No, Mommy, I want to stay with you and my brothers and . . . " She didn't say any more. We sat there together in silence for a few moments, and then she sang to me a song she sometimes lullabied over my bed when I couldn't sleep during thunderstorms: "M–m–m–m–m . . . It's going to be all right. . . ." I lay against her and cried in defiant silence. I didn't want new clothes and college. I wanted to be home in Creighton Court with my family.

Soon the voices of my aunt and uncle floated up through the still night air to where I had shut myself in the bedroom. Mama was making small talk, waiting for me to answer her call for me to come downstairs, but I couldn't move. My legs were pulled up tight against my chest, molding my body into a ball on the bed. My eyes were fixed on the crack dividing the far wall into halves. My safe little world was spinning out of control as if I was on a merry-go-round.

"Kay, darling." It was Mama. Her voice was softer than I had ever heard it. It sounded as smooth and gentle as the velour coverings on the pews in church. She pulled me up on my knees, and we sat on the bed looking swollen eye to swollen eye.

"Little boys can play in the gutter and get up the next morning, put on a clean shirt, and nobody thinks anything of it, because they're boys. A little girl . . ." She paused and touched me gently on the cheek. "A little girl can play in the gutter and get up the next morning, and everybody remembers. And I want you out of this gutter. This is an opportunity for you. I'm still your mama and I will always be your mama, but you're going to take advantage of these opportunities. They're going to give you things that I can't give you."

"Yes ma'am," I answered between sniffles, and I packed my few things and went downstairs. I never questioned my mother's love for me. I trusted her completely, but my heart ached at the thought of leaving my family and neighbors and everything that my small world contained at that time. But Sue Coles had spoken, and I obeyed.

The scene downstairs in the living room could only be described as a study in contrasts. For every cry I swallowed, Aunt Pearl let her joy shine through. She was ecstatic, and even Uncle J. B. had difficulty subduing his elation at seeing me come down the stairs with my bag. I hugged each of my brothers good-bye, pausing a bit when I came to Tony. *He is so young to be left without his playmate*, I thought. As the Chrysler pulled away, I watched through blurry eyes as Creighton Court melted into Nine-Mile Road. And then I wiped my tears and turned to look straight ahead.

We went directly to the Sears store, where I was outfitted with an entirely new wardrobe. Panties, slips, dresses, socks, nothing was left out. At my new home, my aunt and I unpacked my new clothes and arranged them in neat rows in my dresser. It felt good to see all the brand-new colors carefully arranged in the drawers. And so I went to bed, feeling like a princess. I didn't have to fight sleep, because no cockroaches crawled across the ceiling in my new house. I stretched my legs out to the edges of the bed, enjoying the coolness of the fresh sheets against my skin and the freedom of not having to jostle with my brothers for leg room or covers. It was so still and quiet that I wouldn't have to hum songs to drown out the sound of hollering in another apartment. I should have been the happiest girl in the world, but for the first time in my life I felt very lonely and very alone. I cried. The more I tried to suck in my sobs, the more my tiny body shook with the heaving motions of my crying. After a while the sobs turned into a low and mournful moan as I cried softly into my pillow until I drifted off to sleep.

• • •

As sad as it was to leave Mama, I had at least two things going for me. First, I was still with family. Pearl and J. B. were not strangers but familiar faces from a wonderful extended family. And in our community it wasn't unusual for family to take care of each other. How I wish this were more true today, especially for the many working mothers who are struggling to provide for their children.

I was also fortunate because Pearl and J. B. had several surprises for me that made the transition a little easier. One of the things I was most excited about was that they were going to wallpaper their home and I got to pick out the wallpaper for my room. That was one of the most exciting things that had happened to me in my short life. I picked out a bubblegum-pink print of ballerinas. For the rest of my time in that house, I lived with pink, fluffy ballerinas all over my walls.

The house had a scary basement that I tried to avoid, but I had to go down there on rainy days 'cause that's where we hung the wash. Off to the left against the wall, there was an old coal bin that took on terrifying shapes in the dark. My aunt made the three of us huddle beside it during thunderstorms. Both my aunt and uncle were deathly afraid of thunderstorms and sent us running to that scary old basement at the first clap of thunder. Today I love thunderstorms. The noisier the better. It probably has something to do with the time one cold winter when my aunt made us go down into the shadowy basement and I swore to myself that I would never be afraid like they were.

There were only three of us in a four-bedroom house, and it took me a long time to get used to having so much space and so much quiet. Eventually the strange house began to feel like home. The largest bedroom was for Pearl and J.B., and I was in the next room with the dancing

ballerinas. The other two rooms were used as a den and as
an office for J. B.'s insurance business. The house had many
new things to explore. I amused myself for hours with the
swinging door in between the dining room and the kitchen.
They also had a pantry that was stocked with food, not just
enough to get you through the week but enough to last
through a whole year, or at least so it seemed to me. The
kitchen looked ultramodern to me, with its gray formica
countertops and linoleum floor. The downstairs held a
living room, a dining room, and a porch that served as a
living room when the house, without air-conditioning,
became unbearably hot. Summer evenings I would serve
Aunt Pearl and Uncle J. B. a lemonade on the porch as they
talked with the Allens on one side and the Flemmings on
the other.

My favorite spot in the house was the corridor passing
beside my uncle's in-home office, a sparse little room off the
back porch. I loved to sit in the hallway and listen to him
practice the speeches that he would deliver to insurance
groups, black business and professional groups, and community groups. He was well-known as a public speaker, and
he was often traveling to other towns to deliver remarks. He
took this role as orator very seriously, even subscribing to
Vital Speeches of the Day, which he used to improve upon his
own speeches.

I remember sitting in countless audiences listening to
him, so puffed up with pride that I thought I would burst if I
couldn't hurry up and clap. Every once in a while, he would
use me in one of his stories, or ask me to stand and be
recognized. I would roll my eyes, and say "Oh, my word!"
and pretend that I hated it. But I loved it. I do the same
thing to my kids today when they're in an audience. And
they do the same act, "Oh, no, she's gonna use me in the
speech again!"

I credit Uncle J. B. for my own love of public speaking,
though I haven't always felt this way about getting up in
front of an audience. I had always been a shy and quiet
child, but Uncle J. B. put me in situations in which I would

have to speak in front of large groups. One event in particular weighed on me. It was the Universal Life Insurance Company's Christmas party, held every year in Charlottesville, Virginia. My uncle required me to bring greetings from the home office, but just thinking about standing in front of the group filled me with terror. Only a few lines were required, but I spent the better part of the late summer and fall thinking about what I was going to say. Somehow, I made it without fainting and eventually grew more comfortable in front of groups. After a few years of this I reasoned that if he was going to make me do this and the audiences seemed to like what I said every year, I might as well just get up there and speak and not worry about it.

It's an attitude that has proved useful.

Other habits began at those Christmas parties as well. I learned that if I smiled and showed with my body language that I was really glad to be at the party and that I really liked everyone there, then they would graciously receive what I said. I wasn't faking. I really did like the people who came to those annual parties. Especially Eugene and Lorraine Williams who, I thought, were the black Ozzie and Harriet. He was the district manager of Universal Life and a close friend of my uncle. Once when I overheard Eugene and Lorraine argue, it nearly broke my heart because I really thought that they had the perfect family. Now that I'm older, and married as well, I know that my impression was accurate after all.

I always felt warm and accepted at the Christmas party, and I tried to convey warm and accepting feelings back to the audience as I spoke. This lesson would come in very handy later in life when I traveled the country to speak about one of the most divisive issues of our day: abortion. In my role as spokesperson for the National Right to Life Committee, I crisscrossed the country to speak to groups about the value of life. As I walked into rooms filled with very agitated and hostile people, I never forgot the importance of conveying my sincere appreciation for having been given the opportunity to speak with them. And although we may have vehemently disagreed about abortion, I really was glad to be there.

It was also at the Christmas party that I picked up my distaste for using notecards. I reasoned that something would come to me when I was up front, and something always did. And what came to me always seemed better than the silly things I wrote out on diary paper during the bus ride to Charlottesville. Nowadays I sometimes use notes, and I seldom read from a manuscript. Because it irks me to have to sit through a talk by a speaker who reads every word from a prepared text, I don't like putting people through that when I speak. I believe in speaking from the heart, in allowing room for inspiration at key moments.

At one of those Christmas gatherings, Eugene spoke to me in a serious voice. "Kay," he began looking like he had just buried his dog, "I want to tell you something important, something I don't want you to forget." (As if I could ever forget anything Mr. Williams told me!) *The only difference between people who succeed in this world and people who fail is that the ones who succeed get up again after they fail.* I nodded my head to let him know I would never forget the words he spoke. I never forgot.

They say that men who have only daughters raise one of them as a son. I think that I was the closest thing my uncle had to a son and that his teaching me the art of public speaking was his way of passing on his trade, his legacy. Perhaps that's why he sat with me in the breakfast nook for hours, helping me to write and practice my campaign speeches for president of the sixth grade.

Those speeches to the sixth graders at Webster Davis were the origins of what my friends now jokingly refer to as my "other self." It was such a stretch for my shy little self to get in front of folks to speak that I developed something of a defense mechanism. I became another person, another little girl. Where I was tender-hearted, shy, and very frightened, the persona I eventually adopted while speaking was confident, earthy, humorous, and emotional. In time, I began to enjoy speaking in front of groups. I loved the rush of swaying the mood of a crowd. If, before I began, I saw bored, vacant faces, I challenged myself, my persona that is, to say something to waken and warm them. And I loved it when they clapped. Not polite, fingers-fanning-fingers but real palm-slapping-palm applause.

I missed my family, but it was a pain that I learned to live with, like a toothache whose dull hurt is so often with you that you learn to ignore it. We still saw one another quite often. My brother Lucky came over on weekends to do heavy cleaning for my aunt. I'd sit and talk to him while he scrubbed floors, washed down the woodwork, or did yard work. The arrangement worked out well for my aunt and uncle, whose professional lives left them little time for such household duties. Peter and Ted cleaned for Mama's other sisters' families, and the pay that the three oldest boys brought in from this work kept the family afloat during those difficult years.

I would learn later that just before I went to live with my aunt, visitors from the welfare agency came to observe our household. They must have noticed on Mama's application for public housing that she had six children to support with no steady employment and no financial support from my father. The state sent her a check every month, but I guess that even the welfare office knew that the meager sum they sent could not sustain a family of seven. We surely would not have been able to make it if it had not been for the pulling together of our extended family. For years Mama lived under the threat that the state might come and divide the family by sending the children to foster homes. It was like a brick she was holding above her head as she treaded water. And its weight was beginning to wear her down. Still, she was determined to keep us together.

My three oldest brothers, who stayed with Mama, went to work at odd jobs to help support the family. It was while earning grocery money for the family that my brothers picked up one of their great loves in life: golf. There was a golf course near Creighton Court where my brothers would go to retrieve golf balls lost or abandoned after an especially poor shot. Seeing how the Glenwood Golf Course was not exactly a mecca for golf pros, my brothers had ample supply of lost golf balls to find among the underbrush and thick weeds. They would bring home pails of grass-stained balls and then wash and scrub them until they shone a brilliant white. They had a steady supply of customers who would look for them at the gate to buy a supply of the cheaper, recycled balls that my brothers sold.

When they entered their teens, Ted, Peter, and Lucky began to caddie for the players. They were in much demand because their strong, wiry frames could hoist a bag on each shoulder. At $1.50 per bag for eighteen holes, they could bring home in excess of ten dollars a day if they could manage two rounds of caddying and had good tippers. They would come home dead-tired but speaking in animated tones of the shots good and bad that they had witnessed that day. They replayed games in their conversation, second-guessing the golfer's choice of clubs. In these relaxed moments, they would snort and chuckle as they relived some of the poorer performances on the fairway that day. Bursts of laughter often filled the room as they finally unleashed the snickers they had sucked down as they deadpanned, "Uh, perhaps a nine iron would be appropriate for this shot."

Ted especially was proud of his earnings. The boys had established a custom early on among themselves that half of whatever they earned went directly to Mama. I could always tell if the boys had had a successful day on the golf course by the way that Ted would walk in the front door. If it fairly burst open with his energy, I knew that Ted would shortly be calling to Mama to come get the family's share of his earnings. He would gently pull her palm till it extended perpendicularly to her tiny body. He would let it hang there expectantly while he raced deep down into his right pocket where he had stuffed her half of the day's wage, and he would solemnly pull out dollar bill after dollar bill to place on her awaiting hand. His eyes shone, and he couldn't contain his smiling pride as he went through this daily ritual.

On days when golfers stayed away from the course, Ted first, and then the others, trudged wearily home. If he had less than three dollars to contribute to Mama's budget, Ted wouldn't even look up as he plunged his hand down his pocket and shoved the wad of bills onto her hand. His shoulders slumped on these days, for he truly wanted to provide for the family with his earnings.

One spring, in the midst of what should have been perfect golfing weather, a cold front came through that shocked all the flowers that had dared to show their colors. It was cold, real cold—so cold that they took to piling coats up on top of the beds again to keep warm at night, but the boys faithfully tromped out to the frost-covered green to hunt for customers. As the story is told, Ted became so distraught over the measly $1.50 he had been able to earn that day that as the caddies turned to leave the course that blustery day, he called out a dare.

"I bet you a dollar apiece that I'll jump into that creek with my clothes on!" Apparently the other caddies didn't realize how crazy my brother Ted was; or maybe they did and wanted to see him freeze, but they all put up their dollar. Sure enough, he took six giant steps and flung himself into the icy waters, dungarees, and all. He came out as quickly as he had jumped in and grabbed their dollars in a swift, sweeping motion and then ran all the way home with his spoils. His grin touched both ears as he stood in a puddle in the kitchen, tenderly holding Mama's protesting hand as he gingerly laid the soaked bills in her palm.

Over a period of time, my brothers developed cordial relations with the men they caddied for, especially a circle of Jewish businessmen who began to ask for my brothers by name. They developed such good relations that when the Jewish golfers, who themselves were often subtly discriminated against, opened their own golf course across town, the Oakhill Golf Course, my brothers switched golf courses, too. One of the men, who owned Richmond Heating and

Equipment, took a strong liking to Ted, who proved to be reliable, quick, and eager to work. He eventually offered Ted a job in his company, but Ted declined because he was still in high school. But Ted's school years were soon cut short.

Mama had been accepting public assistance off and on throughout our early years to make ends meet. In those days, a welfare recipient was a little higher than a cockroach and equally mistrusted. Every bit of aid that was given had several strings attached to it.

Some of the restrictions were intrusive and downright humiliating. The most notorious and resented were the surprise inspections conducted by social workers looking for signs of a man living in the home. Welfare was intended for widows and wives with children who had been abandoned by their husbands, but during the '50s and '60s, a new profile of welfare recipients began to emerge. They were divorced, separated, or never-married mothers who may or may not have had a continuing relationship with their children's father or fathers.

This new and growing class of welfare recipients created a bit of anxiety in the human service agencies, who wanted to make sure that only the truly needy were receiving public aid, for theoretically, it was possible for single mothers to live with their child's father and still collect welfare money from the state. The government decided that the best way to uncover welfare fraud and abuse was to conduct surprise visits to recipients' homes to see if there were signs of a man living there. During these visits, the social workers would also question the mother about any expensive-looking items in the home.

Ted was home from school one day with a nasty cut on his foot that he had gotten while playing sandlot football, barefoot. That fateful day a social worker from the city came calling. He knew who she was as soon as he opened the door. Social workers were just about the only white folks who ever came to Creighton Court. She didn't ask to come in, she just pushed him aside and began her search. Mama kept her composure through all the questions about the men's clothing in the house. "I have five sons," she replied quietly. But when the woman went into her bedroom and started looking under the bed and in her closet, Mama began to softly weep.

Ted couldn't stand it. Though it hurt him to even move his foot, let alone stand upon it, he walked into the bedroom and pulled the social worker out by the crook of her elbow. He dragged her through the living room and down the steps as Mama followed along behind yelling at her fool son to leave the welfare woman alone. The social worker was in a fit of fury by the time Ted got her to the front steps, and she turned to shout as she walked across our spotless front lawn. "I'm gonna cut you off, just you wait and see, you ungrateful boy! I will cut you off." And she huffed down Nine-Mile Road.

Inside, Mama couldn't calm down Ted enough to make him stop walking on his hurt foot. He kept pacing the halls, sprinkling the concrete floor with his blood, forcefully telling himself and her, "We don't need them, Mama. Ain't no one gonna treat you like that. We'll make it without them." And we did. The family never received another welfare check after that day.

Once his foot healed, Ted never went back to school. He found the generous businessman on the golf course and asked him if his offer of a job was still good. Was it ever! He was hired that week as an air-conditioner installer. It was a good job and paid well. I don't think that I've ever seen anyone as proud as Ted when he received his first paycheck and plopped fives and tens, not ones, down on Mama's palm.

He shocked quite a few folks in Richmond when he showed up to install their new air conditioner. A handful of families flat out refused to have a Negro do the job. The first time it happened, Ted got back in the truck and returned to the factory to let his boss know that he would have to send someone else to that particular home. But his boss told my brother that if there were people who didn't want Ted to install their air conditioner, then he didn't want their business. And the order was canceled.

My other brothers picked up their seasonal work in the same manner. They began the first hole, carrying clubs, but by the eighteenth hole they had usually landed some type of work with the golfer. But no one was able to get a job that paid like Ted's. Often when he was out installing someone's system, he would get a radio call from the owner to return to the shop for a special project. The owner would meet him at his car and they'd head off to the golf course to shoot a few holes on company time. Saturdays, Ted would go over to his boss's home and cut the grass and drive the kids around to dance lessons and baseball games.

With the money Ted earned from his many jobs, he was soon to the point where he could afford to move into his own place, but he didn't. Not yet. He waited until Peter, the second in line, had finished school and secured a job before he left. In turn, Peter did the same thing, waiting until Lucky had graduated and found a job, before moving on.

During this time, Mama went every day to serve as an assistant to one of her sister's husbands, who was a dentist. So, between my brothers' taking any work available to bring money home to Mama, Mama's working for her brother-in-law, and the three youngest children staying with aunts and uncles, we were able to break away from public assistance and the family was able to avoid being split up by the State.

Even with the threat of their children being farmed out to foster families, which threat hung over their lives like an ominous cloud, my parents had decidedly mixed feelings about my brothers' and my going to live permanently with aunts and uncles. Especially my father. But he acquiesced with one strange condition: My Aunt Pearl and Uncle J. B. could take me in only if they agreed to legally adopt me. Mama would hear nothing of it, and the issue became the source of several bitter arguments between my parents. In the black community, the temporary taking in of children in need is a fairly common occurrence, but in my case, my father was against this sort of informal adoption. My brothers later explained to me that my father feared that my childless aunt and uncle only wanted to play at being parents; that they would play with me and spoil me as a child, but then grow tired of the game and send me back later. He wanted to make sure that if they took me on that they would educate me and provide for me and that I would get everything I would be entitled to as a "daughter." Well, Mama refused to "give me up" and Dad lost the argument. I was never formally adopted, but I lived with my aunt and uncle from that point until I left for college at age eighteen.

These were to be years of pain and struggle for me. Years of growth. During these schoolgirl days, my eyes were opened to the dividing lines of American society. I became aware that there were haves and have-nots, niggers and white folks, professionals and servants, men and women. I questioned why God had ordained that I was to be born on the weaker side of every one of the lines I discovered. For the first time, I saw how the other half lived, and I realized that when we all lived together at Creighton Court, we were desperately poor. And I heard day after day that we Coles were the black sheep of the family.

In those formative years, I made the startling discovery that I was black. I was black and the majority of America was white. I went from being totally oblivious to race to being acutely aware of it. In college I would discover that I was black and proud, but before I reached that point came a childhood of painful rejection and hurt. These discoveries came when I was removed from an environment that for all its cockroaches and material want was still a sheltered existence.

chapter six

THE HOTHOUSE

THERE WAS IN THE EARLY FIFTIES a firm conviction among black folks that education was an avenue to freedom. It was not just the educated who held this view, but even the unlettered among us viewed education as our race's highway to equality. Mothers, fathers, grandparents, neighbors, pastors, everyone took an interest in your schoolwork. This academic focus was heightened in my case because my aunt was a schoolteacher herself. For the past ten years she had taught a fourth-grade class at Webster Davis Elementary School in Fulton, a section of the city of Richmond. Every morning I tagged along with her to attend Webster Davis rather than the school near our house.

The environment of Webster Davis wrought quite a change in me from the time I entered Junior Primary 1 to when I graduated from the sixth grade. Of all the adjectives used to describe me today, I don't think that anyone has ever chosen the word "passive." As a black, evangelical, pro-life Republican, my life could hardly be described as a placid existence. As I like to tell my kids, if you want to stand up for your convictions, even when those beliefs pit

you against powerful groups and people, you've got to learn
to eat problems for breakfast.

As a child, though, I was so nonconfrontational that in
the first grade I sat there and let a little girl cut off one of my
braids. That night, staring at the bushy nub that marked the
place where my shoulder-length braid had been, Aunt Pearl
asked incredulously, "Why'd you let her do that? Why
didn't you say anything?" I still don't know the answer to
that question, but something almost mystical happened
during the six years I spent at Webster Davis, and by the
time I reached the sixth grade I was president of the student
body.

Who were the people who taught me to think for
myself and speak out my convictions? Who were the people
who taught me to diagram sentences, memorize Psalm 23,
and hold my head up high? They were teachers like Mrs.
Hembry, Mrs. Mitchell, Mr. Kemp, and Mrs. Hubbard.
They were people like Mrs. Watkins in the office. Much of
the transformation can be attributed to people like Elsie
Lewis, the principal of Webster Davis. Today, when I think
of a black educator, I think of Elsie Lewis.

In the 1950s there were few opportunities for educated
blacks to get jobs in business and industry and government,
so it was not unusual to have black teachers with Ph.D.s
teaching elementary school. Our segregated junior high
schools used secondhand textbooks, but a black man with a
Ph.D. in chemistry taught science class.

At that point in my life I had had so little firsthand
experience with white folks that my understanding of them
came almost entirely from my teachers. They made me
understand that white folks were given all the breaks and
advantages and that we had to be better than them to be
treated equally. We were told in no uncertain terms by these
black teachers that we had to be twice as good and twice as
smart to survive. I can recall as though it were yesterday,
my sixth grade teacher Mrs. Waltz, pointing her ramrod-
straight arm up the hill to the white elementary school,
Fulton Hill. "Those kids are going to be waiting for you

when you get out of here," she would intone, and with eyes flashing she would add, "And you are going to be ready!'

At Webster Davis you never heard children complaining to their teachers that such-and-such was not fair. We knew that such objections would get us nowhere. "Life is not fair" I heard many a teacher snap, "and so don't go looking for fair." We accepted the inherent difficulties and injustices of life as we accepted the stifling humidity of Richmond summers. We didn't like it, and we stiffened our resolve to fight against it, but we conditioned ourselves to persevere and thrive in spite of it. And we knew with a knowing so deep that they must have seasoned the water fountains with it, that life was going to be tough. We never expected it to be easy. No one at Webster Davis, or in the black community at large, ever led us to believe that we could expect to get anything in life that we didn't sweat, bleed, and work for.

But even as our teachers painted us a realistic picture of black life in the fifties, they held up examples of those who had gone before us who had triumphed when the world was even more unfair. They filled our heads with the lyrical prose of James Baldwin. We read biographies of bold and courageous Harriet Tubman and Nat Turner, and the ingenious George Washington Carver. Their realism didn't discourage us. It encouraged us to succeed and flourish and overcome.

I'm thankful that I never encountered one of those "enlightened" teachers, so common in our universities and civic groups these days, who fill young minds so full of the wrongs done to them that young persons become overwhelmed at the thought of overcoming. You can easily recognize their disciples. They're the ones so preoccupied with injustice that they wait all their life for somebody to give them something. They just can't shake the feeling that they're owed something. You've probably met folks like that, men and women whose whole identity revolves around being a victim. Modern psychologists now understand the wisdom of black elders who, in the face of oppression and injustice, preach that we are *survivors*, not victims. "Victims" of sexual abuse, economic exploitation, or racial injustice who fixate on the crimes committed against them are likely to develop a fatalistic, passive stance towards life. "Survivors," notwithstanding, acknowledge the injustice done to them and move on to take control of their destiny.

At Webster Davis we learned that we were part of a proud race of survivors. If I tried to explain away my not doing my algebra homework because of the heavy weight of years of slavery, a heavy weight would soon come down on my behind.

These lessons were reinforced at home with a religious fervor. Every day when I came home from school, I was required to spread out my books in the alcove off the kitchen that my aunt called the "breakfast nook." There I would sit and pore over my lessons, hour after hour. I always had two companions sitting with me as I worked: Aunt Pearl and her can of beer. I would usually begin these homework sessions with English, my favorite subject, and save math for last. I had a very definite reason for doing so. My aunt would look over every assignment I completed, checking for errors, and making sure that the quality was up to her standards. This review was usually helpful during the first three quarters of an hour, but by the time the last two or three subjects came around, Pearl would be so tipsy that she did little more than ramble and berate me for my stupidity.

She would crumple up my math homework and screech at me that I had done them all wrong. I would simply have to start all over and do the problems correctly. That's why I saved math for last. The problems were easy enough to check in my head so I could know for sure that my answers were correct. I would redo the problems again and again, each time Pearl insisting that I was such an "ignorant fool" that I had answered every one wrong, until eventually she would relent and say that I'd finally gotten them right. We went through this routine every afternoon and evening. I was a prisoner there at that table, and I was forced to sit there long after all my assignments were finished until Aunt Pearl finally announced bedtime.

In sixth grade I had my first encounter with the kind of black woman whose presence caused even the scraggly bean plants growing in the egg cartons in the window to stand straight. Our classroom could hardly contain the energy of Mrs. Wolfes. That woman would aggravate the fire out of me. She demanded so much. Hardly a day went by that either her lessons or her homework didn't leave me with a red-rubbed callus on my writing finger. But her attention to detail, her insistence on excellence, nourished my soul. Her exacting standards waged a silent war with the messages of a hostile society that I had internalized and believed, without realizing it: that I was worthless, inferior, lazy, and dumb.

Between Aunt Pearl and Webster Davis, my head was so packed full of learning by the end of the school year that I was desperate for summer to come. Summer camps are an invention of modern times to give urban kids a chance to get out of the city and go experience the joy of life in the country. When we were growing up, black kids didn't need summer camps because everyone had family in the country. During the 1940s and 1950s, hundreds of thousands of black folks had migrated from sharecropping farms in the South to industrial centers in the North. Enterprising, bold black men and their families packed up their few belongings and headed north to cities like Detroit, Michigan, Gary, Indiana, and New York City, to fill what were considered well-paying factory jobs. Many of the established farmers and older folks stayed in the country, though.

After school let out, the exodus began as kids were shipped out to spend the season with any kin that remained in places like North Carolina, Georgia, Mississippi, and even as far as Texas. When we came back together in the fall, the neighborhood kids would trade stories about milking cows, castrating hogs, and building forts in the woods. Nowadays, with family ties not what they once were, parents either have to buy that kind of experience for their children or they do without. It's a shame. I know that today I certainly wouldn't feel comfortable calling up my second cousin twice-removed to send my kids to their home for two months, but that was accepted practice in my childhood.

We were lucky. My uncle J.B. had a brother and a sister who lived nearby in New Kent County. Every summer we spent weekends and odd days at their farm. My relatives in New York City sent their kids down for the entire summer. We city kids relished the playgrounds that Mother Nature had created for our cousins. The country was a world of wonder for those of us who thought that milk came from a truck and that vegetables grew in supermarkets. We caught tadpoles in the brook and climbed trees and chased rabbits.

Meals in the country were a celebration. The food was good and plentiful. They ate Sunday dinner every day: fresh vegetables, succotash, ham, peach pie, and other things that we ate only on special occasions at home. The exercise, fresh air, and Southern home cooking left me healthy and refreshed for another school year. It also provided a desperately needed break from the demands of living up to Aunt Pearl's expectations.

All too soon it was time to return to Richmond and the rigors of school. But I wouldn't have wanted it any other way. During my years at Webster Davis school, using secondhand textbooks and borrowed typewriters, I was stretched academically as I would never be again. My future years of schooling would hold challenges of a different nature, but my time at Webster Davis was an unparalleled learning experience. I knew from growing up that there are certain things that can be said and done among family that can't be said and done when company's over. In our separate school, among family, we were pruned and trimmed to blossom in our season. Webster Davis was a hothouse, a closed environment where our teachers could turn up the heat. The heat was so high at times it made us sweat with the effort, but we grew.

I thrived in that separate world in which my abilities

and potential weren't called into question on account of my skin color. Expectations were high. No excuses were accepted. I was expected to know the answer and when I didn't, *I could do better than that!*

Looking back, I am very thankful for that time in the hothouse, for it strengthened my roots and extended my branches and, in general, prepared me for a time when I would be transplanted to a foreign soil within my own country—white-people-land. Had it not been for those nurturing years, I may very well have wilted and faded under the scorching heat of racial injustice that I would soon experience in white America.

chapter seven
TOSSING THE SALAD

MY CLOTHES FOR MY FIRST DAY of junior high school had been carefully ironed and starched. My brand-new saddle shoes were a gleaming black and white, without a single crease in the leather. Pearl and I spent a long time picking out just the right dress to convey an image of confidence and taste. However, the seeping stains under my arms belied the anxiety within. I was more nervous on my first day at Chandler Junior High School than I had been leaving for Junior Primary One. We were going from being the leaders of grade school to lowly seventh graders.

Even worse, some man had taken the school system to court, and the judge had decided that schools should be integrated. The weight of that decision for the future of my race concerned me little. I was preoccupied with what that man who had sued the school was getting me into. I wondered why integration meant that black students were thrust into white territory, to learn new diction, new customs, and new ways of doing things. Integration *never* meant that white girls left their friends and neighborhoods to attend a black school like Webster Davis.

I left home with Pearl calling out the door for the

twentieth time that morning: "You remember your manners now—*Please* and *Thank-you* to your teachers!"

"Yes, ma'am, I'll remember," I called back. Her nervousness made me grow even more anxious. I carried a feeling with me on the walk to school, like the flutter in your stomach on the way up the highest summit of a roller coaster track. My car had been climbing higher and higher, ever since my aunt informed me I would be going to a white school. And now I was poised to roll over the top of the curve and zoom down the terrifying slope.

Life had been relatively peaceful inside my all-black enclave. Frankly, this tossing of the proverbial salad bowl of American cultures was an unwelcome nuisance. On May 17, 1954, the U.S. Supreme Court outlawed segregation in public schools. For many years the legal ruling was simply ignored. President Eisenhower's order that troops escort students to school in Little Rock, Arkansas, was the first signal that integration would soon be enforced.

Virginia's Democratic political machine, run by Senator Byrd, vowed to fight any attacks on the fine Southern tradition of segregation of the races. Their strategy was named Massive Resistance: The governor would close any school the courts ordered to desegregate. A Pupil Placement Board was established with the authority to approve student and teacher applications for transfers and assignments. For a long time this board sabotaged local efforts by groups like the NAACP to integrate the schools. Finally in 1960, some two hundred black students were approved to transfer to white schools. These brave children were sent out in groups of twos and threes to integrate schools where they were outnumbered a hundred to one. Two eighth graders integrated Chandler, a school picked for its strategic location on the edge of the middle-class black and white sections of Richmond's North Side.

Richmond was in a fury. Angry residents complained of falling property values if blacks were seen in their neighborhood. Some parents were so apoplectic at the thought of their kids sitting beside black children that they withdrew their children from public schools. There was talk of "blood flowing in gutters." The next year I was one of twenty-six black students approved by the Pupil Placement Board to join the incoming class of three hundred white students at Chandler in what one Richmond paper has described as "one of the most ambitious experiments in race-mixing the South had seen."

I didn't feel particularly ambitious that first day. I felt intimidated and overwhelmed. I walked softly down the halls, my head turned down, intimidated by the older kids towering above me. In the hallways I backed my skinny, undeveloped body against the wall so that I did not have to answer the conceited stares of the girls who had sprouted breasts and the boys who smoked cigarettes behind the school dumpster. If my time at Webster Davis could be described as challenging, nurturing, and caring, my next six years spent integrating the schools could be described, in part, as dehumanizing, alienating, and cruel.

My concentration in class was disturbed by the resonating tick of the classroom clock, which seemed to announce that the time for another pass through the hallways was quickly approaching. Before I had finished tucking my books under my arm and headed out the threshold, my stomach was already knotted up inside in dread anticipation of my fellow students. Hallways were a chaotic swirl of students changing classes. The always noisy, always frantic corridors provided cover for white bullies. For the first month, I never made it from one class to the next without at least one student's pricking me with a pin. Sometimes I was stuck so many times I had to press my dress against my body to keep the red streams from dripping down my legs. I tried to be discreet. I didn't want them to know that their taunts or their jabs hurt me.

At first I couldn't tell one white student from the rest. No kidding! They all looked and dressed pretty much the same. I didn't bother to learn their names. Even the ones who didn't jab us never talked to us anyway. The black kids had been spread out one or two to a class. We sought each other out during lunch and sat together in one big black clump. That was the only time I felt safe. The rest of the day was a fearful and lonely existence.

Perhaps my greatest fear was being caught alone in the hallway with one of the white toughs who took special joy in threatening us. One day it happened. I was descending the large stairway in Chandler's front hall when a group of white kids started up. Most of them ignored me as I tried to inconspicuously step down the side. One of them waited till my back was turned and pushed me, hard, down the stairs. I landed at the end with my shins and back bruised. Apparently it wasn't enough for him, so he kicked my books all over the hall as well. The crowd laughed and made jokes.

And then an amazing thing happened. One of the faceless, nameless white girls in the crowd stepped out and began helping me gather my books. She continued even as her friends turned on her and called her "nigger lover." Unfazed, she walked me down the hall to the office. She didn't say much, but she said enough to make it clear that the boy who pushed me spoke and acted for himself, and not all white people. That may have been the single most important incident in shaping my views on race.

Hallways were scary, but once into my next class I could breathe a sigh of relief. I instinctively trusted the teachers, hoping that in their maturity they would offer a sort of haven from the abuse we suffered from the white kids. I made a conscious effort to sit close to the front where my teachers could see that I was sitting up straight, paying attention, and ready to answer their questions. I had even begun to allow myself to relax a little in their presence. One day during the slack time in homeroom my eyes followed the dancing of a blue jay out the second-story windows. I paid half-attention to Mrs. Osborne who was dutifully reading off the menu. "Today we're having grilled cheese sandwiches, vegetable soup, milk, cookies, and brownies for dessert." At this point she paused and looked over her glasses at me and added for the class's enjoyment, "And heaven knows why they're having brownies. We have enough of them here already."

That remark stung more than the pinpricks I had received passing through the halls. I expected to face ridicule and abuse from the students, but I had imagined that if things ever got really bad, we could go to the teachers who would protect us and take care of us. But I was a "brownie" in Mrs. Osborne's eyes, and there was no safe haven at John Chandler.

Fortunately, my years at Webster Davis had instilled in me enough confidence in my academic ability that the D's and F's on my papers during my first year at Chandler only served to make me work harder. It was their ploy to discourage us. They would grade our papers harder than our white classmates and hold up our failures for the entire class to see how silly it was to think that black children could compete with white students.

Once the black community became aware of this roadblock on the avenue, they mobilized to overcome it. Parents, pastors and neighbors set up tutoring programs and sought outside assistance to help us survive. Once the teachers saw that we were not easily discouraged, they began to grade our papers more impartially. And my grades, once the weight of bias was removed, rose to their natural level of A's and B's, like a submerged cork buoying up to the surface of the water.

I went on to John Marshall High School where things were not significantly different. Life at home was often worse. The smell of alcohol on my aunt's breath had become such a habitual smell that to this day the reek of stale beer floods my mind with memories of life at Aunt Pearl's. We got along fabulously, the two of us, when she was sober. She could be kind, generous, and fun to be with. And she was so dedicated to her teaching that she never once went to school tipsy, or reeling from a hangover.

But every day after school Pearl would begin drinking, and the perfect Armistead would soon become another person. "Ka–ay, you come in here right now, y' hear!" she would call, and I'd grudgingly follow the sound of her slurred speech into the kitchen. In those hours of drunken stupor, tensions that hid themselves under busyness during the workday would surface and find their outlet. It was during these after-school tirades that we had our most candid conversations, or I should say, I heard her most honest thoughts.

One of her favorite topics during her drunken diatribes was "that Coles blood" in me. Curiously, when she was sober, she never mentioned my father, nor did a disparaging word about any of my family cross her lips. But when the bottle had had its way with my aunt, I learned the depth of her animosity toward my father.

As I got older and passed from junior to senior high, her tongue-lashings got meaner. She was a vicious drunk. "You aren't going to amount to a thing! The Coles blood in you is going to ruin you! Bitch! You little Coles whore!" I learned most of what I knew about rebellion from her explicit fantasies about the things that I was supposedly doing in my spare time. "You stumbling around like you've been drinking!" she'd spew at me, her breath covering my face with an alcohol cloud. "And I smell smoke on you, too, you sorry little cheat. You been smoking cigarettes with those boyfriends of yours, now ain't you?"

At times she would become so agitated as she mulled over my imagined sins that she would kick me out of the house. One time when my uncle was out of town—and it was always worse when he was traveling—Aunt Pearl went into my closet and threw all of my clothes out in the front yard and put me out like a cat on the doorstep.

Sometimes when her tantrums were especially bad I would go to live with my brother Pete and his new wife, who lived across town in a cozy two-bedroom apartment. Other times my aunt would angrily call my mother, or one of my father's relatives, and demand that they come pick up the "little Coles whore" living in her home.

It occurred to me one Saturday, as I was holed up in my room, that I might as well indulge myself in a little fun. I was going to be punished for drinking, smoking, and carrying on whether I did it or not. So why not have a little fun? *Since I have carte blanche to be a bad kid*, I reasoned, *I might as well enjoy some of these things Aunt Pearl is convinced that I'm doing.* I had a few friends at school whose decadent lifestyles could outperform even Pearl's illustrious imagination. It would be a relatively simple thing to join in some of their rebellion.

But something held me back. Call it pride, call it a sense of heritage. Maybe it was God's protection. But I just couldn't bear the thought of having Mama find out. I determined then that I was going to prove Aunt Pearl wrong. "I am a Coles," I told my dresser filled with Aunt Pearl's gifts, "and I am not that kind of person."

And so I continued as the kid who seldom did anything wrong, and it resulted in nicknames like "goody two-shoes" and "granny goodwitch" from my classmates. I was so careful about being good that I made my own self sick! But I was proving something to the voices in my mind. Strange enough, it wasn't the thick Southern voices choked with hate that kept resounding in my mind. It wasn't the voice of the white man on the bus who had called me "dirty nigger" that I was rallying against. I knew that those white racists were just misguided fools, as my mother had explained. But another voice accusing me of being no-good played constantly in my mind. It was a husky voice with the snap of a black woman that I fought to disprove. And so when classmates pointed a bottle my way, inviting me to take a drink, my hand would not reach out to take it. I was tempted; its warm glow promised to dull my aching soul. But I would not allow myself to numb my raw hurt with its power.

I think that I also instinctively knew that avoiding the party scene during high school protected me from a lot more than just Pearl's wrath. It also earned the respect and attention of two white girls, Beth and Martha. Just about the only times white and black kids mixed at our integrated school was when we were forced to sit in alphabetical order.

That was how I, Kay Coles, came to sit between Beth Boswell and Martha Delaney.

Beth and Martha were bosom buddies. Seating charts had placed them together since elementary school when they would call each other up on the phone and plan their matching outfits for the next day. When I was first assigned to sit between them, they tried to carry on their normal conversations by leaning either forward or backward in their seats. I'd feign indifference as I tasted every morsel of their whispered words. I was curious to hear what white girls talked about when they confided in each other's ear. I was surprised to learn that their conversations sounded an awful lot like talks between black girls: "Did you see what Todd is wearing today?! Jenny is trying out for cheerleading! Can you believe that fat girl is going to put on one of those skirts? Are you going to the sorority meeting?" Of course black girls wouldn't be talking about their plans for joining the school sororities, or the cheerleading squad, or the band for that matter. During those early years black students weren't included in a school's extracurricular activities.

Martha would say just about anything in front of me. She didn't curtail her conversations at all in my presence. She would lean her freckled arm on my desk and talk directly to Beth, pausing her voice only when it seemed that someone in an adjacent desk was listening, or one of the teachers chastised her for talking. At first I thought that this may be a sign that Martha liked me, but I came to realize that in her mind, I was just like the desk, a piece of furniture in the way. It never entered her mind to guard her speech in front of me, because it also never entered her mind that a *person* was listening.

Beth, however, seemed always aware of my presence, though she didn't quite know what to make of me. One day, out of the corner of my eye, I caught Beth studying me as we finished our geometry. My faced flushed hot and I was glad for my caramel color that didn't broadcast to the world when I was flustered, like the red-faced white kids. I kept my gaze straight ahead and pretended not to notice. Then, in the next period, she passed me a note. I was used to accepting notes from Beth and passing them to Martha, and vice versa, but this was different. It was addressed to me! My eyes locked on the bubbly letters spelling out my name. Kay. There it was, no confusing it with Martha. I shot a glance over in Beth's direction to see what kind of game she was playing. But there was no mischievous look in her eye as she scribbled down notes from the blackboard.

Inside she wrote, "Hi! Isn't this class boring? I like your dress. —Beth." I couldn't believe it. Beth Boswell had sent me a note! Not only that, she had paid me a compliment. I was vaguely aware of an amazed Martha on the other side of me trying to read what Beth had written.

I quickly refolded the note so that a blank space faced up and wrote back, "Hi! Thanks for the note. If you think this class is bad, I heard we're doing opera again in music class! —Kay." Not to be outdone, Martha soon wrote me a note. As she passed me the note, she caught my gaze and looked deeply into my eyes. I swear that it was the first time that she had ever taken notice of me. I think it surprised her to see a person looking back at her through those dark eyes.

• • •

And so began a friendship among the three of us. We chatted away during class and passed notes when the teachers reprimanded us for talking. We sat together in library, even though there were no assigned seats, and did our homework together on the wide tables. Beth and Martha were the first white people I had ever spent enough time with to really get a good look at their faces. Sometimes I would ask them questions just so that I could study their features as they talked. Their faces amazed me. Their noses were thin and pointy and sprinkled with freckles. White girls, I discovered, could have pink lips without wearing lipstick. Beth had long, flowing hair that was a golden corn color on top but darker, almost brown, underneath. Martha had dark, curly tresses that frizzed up when the rain caught her without a hat. She was covered with freckles from head to toe, and I was tempted to ask her, though I never did, if we could play connect-the-dots on her arms. Beth sometimes wore her hair back in a braid, sort of a corn-row done inside out. But poor Beth, hers was difficult hair to braid, and by the end of the school day her hair had usually fallen into a loose knot on her neck. White people smelled different, too, like the inside of the ice cream parlor, sort of sugary sweet and unreal.

In homeroom class, we would compare our homework and help each other out if one of us had skipped an assignment. During these times, Beth and Martha would fill me in on any news that had developed after school the day before, for they were always over at one another's house when school let out. I considered it only a matter of time before they trusted me to be a part of their after-school play. I knew that soon they would invite me over for their slumber parties, or to go horseback riding with their families on weekends. I remember one Monday morning when Beth came in our homeroom class in an excited swirl. She could hardly wait to tell me about the weekend they had had at the beach.

"Oh, Kay, we had such a wonderful time! You should have seen Martha trying to jump over the waves with me. And we ate cotton candy on the boardwalk—it was like eating sweet spider webs!" And then she would plop down in her seat, breathless in her excitement at reliving their magical weekend. I held my breath as she finished her delicious description, waiting for her to add, "Kay, you just must come with us next time!"

But it never came. I was never invited to share in their fun times.

At first it hurt me, and then it made me angry. And then I accepted the fact that we could be good friends at school but not after school hours. I wouldn't know such feelings of hurt and rejection again until I joined an integrated church.

• • •

On the home front, Aunt Pearl was as predictable as ever. Cordial and friendly when sober, ornery when drunk. I never really second-guessed my mother's decision to send me to live with my aunt, but there were times when I wondered if it would have been better staying with Mama. An unexpected turn of events, however, gave me another opportunity to live with Mama and yet still enjoy the creature comforts of Aunt Pearl's home: Mama came to live with *us*. It was a family decision really. A nasty fall sent Grandmother Armistead to the hospital where she was to be in traction for an extended period. Once it became clear that Gramma, as we called her, would be in the hospital for quite a spell, the Armistead sisters decided that someone needed to tend to her there, to make sure that she was cared for. Mama was the natural choice for the position, she being the only nonprofessional among the group. And everyone chipped in to make up the salary she had lost by leaving my uncle's practice. That arrangement lasted long past the humid summer and into the winter.

Near Christmas, Gramma was finally well enough to go stay with another daughter, Etna. However, the weeks of immobility in the hospital had left her unable to move without great difficulty and pain. Mamma took care of Gramma during the day while Etna and her husband were working. At another family meeting, it was decided that Mama should continue to care for Gramma in Etna's home. So, in a sense, my mother became her sister's domestic. We didn't see it that way. We saw it as everybody working together to make it all fit.

Things fit together even more strangely when I was in high school, and Aunt Etna died of cancer. Gramma then came to live with Aunt Pearl. Mama loved this time with her mother, her sister, and her daughter all in one house. She saw it as her opportunity to do things for me that she never had a chance to do while I was growing up. She hummed church songs as she ironed my blouses, organized my dresser drawers, and fixed snacks for me when I came home from school. I especially loved hearing Mama's voice as she sang those songs from church.

I was on familiar terms with God, having grown up accustomed to hearing my mother call upon his name almost daily. God was a kindly old grandfather figure who swept in and out of your life at key moments like birth, baptism, marriage, and death. But I wasn't much of a prayer, except when I was in trouble, and then I could be quite eloquent. Aunt Pearl made sure that she, J. B., and I went to Mt. Carmel Baptist Church once a quarter whether we needed to or not.

The affirmation, inspiration, courage, and pride that we learned at church on Sunday was at odds with an outside world that told us we were second-class citizens, stupid, lazy, and worse. Inside the walls of the church, I heard that I was God's beloved child, created in his image. And this instilled in me a sense of my own inherent worth and dignity that nothing in my experience with white America could destroy. The church also taught me that hate destroys the human spirit, but love builds it up. This and other truths I would call upon in future years.

Part of the magnetic draw of the black church was the warm fellowship. It was one of very few places where "our kind" could go to find love, acceptance, and that most scarce of all commodities, respect. The black man who knelt Monday through Saturday at other men's feet, huffing and sawing his arms in constant motion to shine their shoes, could walk proudly to church on Sunday, knowing that the only one he would be kneeling for that day was the Lord. A janitor could spend all week cleaning up others' trash and, come Sunday, be the respected head of the Ushers' Board. The mass of black women employed as domestics looked forward to two days out of the week: Thursday, their day off, and Sunday, which was the Lord's day. Imagine the pride of the woman who spent all week cooking and cleaning for a white family but, come Sunday, headed up the women's Missionary Board. A spirit of kinship and community rolled over the church as the choir director called out lines from the worn hymnals. "Lining" songs is a tradition as old as the black church in America, a remnant from the days when most of the congregation couldn't read.

I loved those Sundays when the choir director included a gospel tune with a snatch of African percussion. I liked the two-four time laments well enough. Particularly as a melancholy child, those "nobody knows the trouble I seen" songs spoke to my heart. But my favorite songs were those that enticed the usually reticent congregation to keep time with foot stomps and claps. When the choir was especially good, the ladies of the church would add a little hop to their clap and the men would open their hands wide apart on every clap and rock back and forth with the pulse. We'd wear out the lyrics, singing them five or six times through until the congregation had worked itself into a frenzy of singing and clapping. Then it would be over and the men would hitch up their pants a notch or two, and ladies would fan their glowing faces, and the whole church would settle into the pews with a satisfied and exhausted *Amen*.

I liked going to church and receiving the warm greetings from other families. Sundays meant new barrettes and having my hair braided tightly against my scalp. It meant crisp dresses and white lace socks with patent leather shoes. The older I became, however, the less sense I could make of what I heard and saw in church. I thought long and hard about the porcelain Jesus hanging limply from the cross on the wall. It often caused my little mind to question how a blue-eyed, blond Jesus could love dark, nappy me. Would there be a section in heaven, in the back near the edges separating heaven from hell, a separate section for us blacks? When we finally slipped the bounds of this earthly world and went to drink living water, would there be one fountain for blacks and one for whites, as we had in Christian America?

The whole business about being a Christian also confused me. It's a fact of life that in tightly knit communities like ours, everybody knows everybody else's business.

It puzzled me that many of those who sang, professed, confessed, and preached on Sunday lived rather unChristian lives the rest of the week. By the time I entered my senior year of high school, I had pretty much decided that Christianity was a great set of rules to govern your life, but that was it. I was a good kid, I always had been, and if God graded on the curve, I'd surely get into heaven.

One evening, J. B., Pearl, and I sat around the kitchen table, eating dinner with the television droning on in the background as it usually did during meals. The show caught my attention. I forgot to eat and sat with my eyes glued to the screen.

"That guy have anything *interesting* to say?" my uncle asked. He was referring to Billy Graham, whose earnest face filled the television screen.

"Mmmm," I replied, concentrating on what Dr. Graham was saying. I'd dialed past televised crusades before without much interest. But this time it seemed that he was talking directly to me! He was speaking to young people about confusion, loneliness, alienation, and fear.

"Do you feel an emptiness in your heart? A lack of purpose and meaning in your life?"

"Yes," I whispered in my heart.

"There is a place in our soul that only Jesus Christ can fill," he explained. I had definitely felt that emptiness!

"Going to church doesn't make you a Christian anymore than going to a garage makes you a car" he said. *Wow!* I thought to myself. *Then what* does *make you a Christian?* Just as if he were reading my mind, Mr. Graham started talking about our need to turn our lives over to Jesus Christ, who would help us be the kind of person we wanted to be.

It sounded great, but I didn't know what it meant to "give my life to Christ." It sounded sort of scary. After dinner I went to my room and prayed. Billy Graham seemed so trustworthy, and I imagined that God would look something like him. I told God that I would give my life to him for a year, to see what would happen.

There weren't any lightning bolts or emotional feelings.

I was kind of disappointed. I certainly didn't feel any different, but I found a Bible and began reading a few chapters every night. I couldn't think of anyone I could share my decision with, so I kept it to myself and studied and prayed on my own. It wasn't long before I noticed changes in myself. I was less concerned with rules and being "perfect" and more concerned with pleasing God. When I did something wrong, I felt a sorrow deep in my heart. Most of all, I had a sense of peace, a calm and a confidence that I had never experienced. It wasn't long before others remarked on the different person I was becoming. I wanted to tell them, "That's because I'm a Christian now," but I never could say it.

chapter eight
THE RADICAL YEARS

T H E   W A R M   F E L L O W S H I P and soul sharpening I experienced in the black church also had the effect of igniting within me a desire to attend a historically black college or university. It was important for me to go to a college where I could be nurtured and protected and challenged by people that I knew cared about me. And I wanted to study in an environment where I was not a minority. I wanted to go somewhere where people understood me, my background, my hair. I wanted to go to a college where I could join the pep squad, the sororities, or the math club if I wanted to.

Not that I had all that much choice. In 1967 there were some opportunities to go to white institutions—not as many as today, but there were a few. Nevertheless, my first choice in schools was Hampton Institute, now called Hampton University, a school known for its excellent education since the days that Booker T. Washington was a student. So the following year I enrolled as a freshman history major at Hampton.

Hampton was perfect for me. It was far enough away from home that I felt a comfortable distance from childhood, yet not too far to return to do laundry every once in a while. Most of the members of my family who had gone to college attended either Virginia Union or Virginia State. Hampton offered me the opportunity to strike out and be independent. As an added bonus I had a few friends who were planning on attending Hampton as well.

It came as a big shock to me that three of my first five professors were white. *I came here to get away from you people!* I thought to myself. Nevertheless, any fears that Hampton would be anything like my junior high or high school were quickly put to rest. This was a time in our nation's history when the country moaned with the imminent birth of the black-power movement. During those years at Hampton I saw the movement come into full bloom. Old ways of thinking and old patterns of doing things were tossed aside in favor of new, radical choices. Black pride was a potent force unleashed on an unsuspecting nation.

After six demeaning years of trying to integrate the schools, I needed those years of affirmation and support. If it took integrating Chandler to make me realize that I was black, it took Hampton for me to realize that I was black and beautiful.

This discovery and celebration of my black identity was intimately related to my discovery and celebration of my identity as a beloved child of God. Up until then, I was the original Lone Ranger Christian. I would hole myself up in my room with my Bible because I was quite sure that I was the only one in the state who was serious about getting to know Jesus and live according to his will. It shocked and amazed me one day, when I was studying at a table at one of the eating facilities at Hampton, to overhear at the table next to me a conversation about God. Students were discussing Jesus' command: ". . . Go and make disciples of all nations." I was astonished, to say the least! Not only were there others like me who were serious about this Christian thing, but they were pretty normal-looking kids— not at all the geeks I had expected to find pouring over the Bible.

That chance encounter began a four year period of fellowship with the InterVarsity Christian Fellowship (IVCF) on campus. It was an unparalleled period of spiritual feeding and growth. I couldn't get enough of the Bible studies, prayer meetings, and worship times that the IVCF staff led with Hampton students.

My growing knowledge of the Bible led me to a greater understanding of who I am in God's eyes. One of my favorite passages during this period was Psalm 139, especially the lines that read:

For Thou didst form my inmost being;
You knit me together in my mother's womb.
I praise you because I am fearfully
and wonderfully made;
Your works are wonderful,
I know that full well.

I am fearfully and wonderfully made! I would tell myself over and over again. And my soul rejoiced to know very well the love my Heavenly Father had for me. It was so freeing, so exhilarating. It was with a sense of childlike wonder that I grasped the fact that God loved even a little nappy-haired girl like me. He actually had knit me together in my mother's womb. He loved me even before I was born!

It wasn't long before it dawned on me that not only had God created me, but He had created me black. A newfound pride in being black sprouted within me. In fact, several of the Christians on campus were leaders in the black-is-beautiful movement. We knew that black is beautiful, and we knew why. God had created us in His image, and God did not create mistakes. He knew what he was doing when He gave us kinky hair, broad noses, full lips, and darker skin. These were beautiful physical features, not traits to be camouflaged in an effort to appear more white.

During this phase I thought a lot about the white blood circulating in my veins that robbed me of some of my color. I began to regret my caramel-color skin, wishing that I had been born tar-colored like some of the African exchange students on campus. We threw away the bleaching creams we had used in high school to make our skin lighter and the processing chemicals to straighten our hair. Both the men and the women in our clique wore their hair in a curly mass known as an "afro." We affectionately termed our hairdo a "natural," because it was naturally who we are. It had been so long since I had let my hair do its thing that I really didn't know how to take care of it. Luckily there was an older girl in our fellowship group who was years ahead of us not only in school but in her black discovery as well. She taught us how to care for our naturals, what combs and gels to use.

Kinte cloth wasn't big then, but if it had been, I would probably have gone to class looking like an African village queen. We called each other "brother" and "sister" and adopted certain catchphrases like "What's happenin'?" and "Right on." Like all young zealots, we also adopted a certain arrogance for our enlightenment. I remember looking down on those Negroes who hadn't yet awakened to the truth. It was as if we had gone through an initiation rite and were only now truly black.

Neither my natural nor my new attitude were much appreciated at home, where they interpreted my actions as a rejection of the way I had been raised. I tried to explain that it was just an affirmation of who I was at the core of my being, the real me, the way God had created me without any alterations to be more acceptable to the predominantly white culture. But I was suspect, and Pearl spread it around the family that I had become a radical.

I had such a wonderful support system from my new family of believers at college that the lack of support from home didn't really bother me a whole lot. For the first time in my life, I felt unconditionally loved and accepted. I felt like I was part of a movement much larger and more important than myself. We fellow black Christians had a saying that summed up our theology: "We're not a minority, we're a chosen few." We "chosen few" made it our business to ensure that we didn't remain few. We learned how to share our faith in Jesus Christ with other students on campus. The fact that Hampton students were culled mostly from the Bible Belt made things harder instead of easier. It is difficult for someone who has been brought up knowing only about God to become interested in knowing God.

The rise in power and prominence of Black Muslims also made our efforts to tell people about Jesus more difficult. Malcolm X and his followers had labeled Christianity "the white man's religion." Those who followed Christ were looked down upon as having sold out to the white establishment. Those were the days of Angela Davis and the Black Panthers, Stokely Carmichael, and college protests. It was the heyday of militant black nationalism, and feelings of black separatism were strong.

Many times I found myself and Scripture agreeing with what the black militants were shouting on campus. I could certainly identify with their vehement opposition to the injustices that white America had for so long forced upon black America. Although I did not agree with their solutions to the turmoil in our nation, I could certainly understand why their message of black power had vast appeal for those who felt alienated and marginalized in America. The call to "Kill whitey!" was a salve for many struggle-weary souls, but our balm was in Gilead.

We began to have debates with them on campus. In short order, the basis of our differences became clear. The militants argued that since white America had made itself rich on our backs, it owed us something. Seeing that the "white devils" would never give us anything willingly, we were going to have to take it—by any means necessary. It was powerful rhetoric. On more than one occasion it was the spark that set a city on fire.

Their beliefs were built on hate, bitterness, and in some cases, I think, fear. Where they advocated substituting black supremacy for white supremacy, I heard Jesus calling for us to forgive and move toward racial reconciliation. To the black militants, "love" and "forgiveness" seemed a show of cowardly weakness. In my mind, if black Americans worked to establish justice for all, it would be the most awesome display of power and love ever witnessed in America.

I'm very glad that my growing years as a Christian took place in that historical context. Following Jesus Christ was not the popular thing to do. The cultural and theological challenges from atheists and Muslims forced me to critically examine the claims of Christ and determine if they were, in fact, true. There was a cost to being a Christian. I endured many taunts and jeers from those who believed that Christianity is the opium that white people use to keep black people happy and content, and "in their place."

I remember an existentialist play that came to campus called "Waiting for Godot." It was one of those plays that you went to see and then retired to a coffee house to discuss the theological and intellectual underpinnings of its dialogue. I had to chuckle during one of our rallies when one of the militant black leaders deliberately mispronounced the name of the play's hero to drive home an emphatic, "Black folks do not have time to wait for no Go-dot." And he was right. We were worried about eating and sleeping and the critical, practical world right here. We didn't have time to sit around and philosophize, waiting for Mr. Go-dot.

The Christians picked up on those themes and agreed, "We do not have time for a feel good religion; something that is just nice to help us get through the day. We have real problems, real needs. We have real questions and we need a God who can address those. We are about looking for truth," we told our non-Christian friends. "If it isn't true, then we don't have time for it. The problems in the black community are so pressing that we don't have time for opium and salves and emotional experiences." Through this kind of one-on-one conversation, the Christians on campus soon became known. There were some who accepted and appreciated us. Many joined us. Others ridiculed and harassed us.

Although I didn't enjoy all the friction at the time, I feel that God was using that time to prepare me for the onslaught of the future. In college I was challenged to think through issues, to think through my faith, figure out if it was real for me, and then be willing to stand by it and take the criticism, take the harassment, take the heat. If that wasn't a preparation for being a leader in the pro-life movement, I don't know what is.

Some of the white folks involved in IVCF at that time, though sympathetic to the black struggle, just could not understand the riot mentality sweeping the nation in the early sixties. I remember trying to explain black rage to white Christian friends. They just couldn't understand it. I understood it, though I couldn't condone it, and I tried my best to be a cultural interpreter for them.

"People don't burn what they own," I tried to explain, "and we've got a whole lot of black Americans in this nation who have been working all their life and don't own a thing. And I don't just mean owning material possessions like a home or a car. I mean that black people in this country don't feel like they have any sense of ownership in our government, in our mayor's office, in the Armed Forces." I would compare the rioters' frustration with the indignation of our Founding Fathers, who over two hundred years ago rebelled against taxation without representation.

"We pay our taxes just like everyone else but have only a handful of black congressmen, generals, and businessmen to represent our interests." It always amazed me how easily my white friends understood and accepted the old adage that "power corrupts," yet they couldn't understand its corollary—that powerlessness corrupts, too.

How do you explain feeling powerless? How do you explain to someone who has so much, who has always looked ahead to a bright future, the feeling of having nothing to lose? How do you explain generations of disappointment and sorrow and struggle and pain? It was difficult, for many times I was at a loss to explain the seemingly senseless destruction of their own community stores and buildings. Self-destructive endeavors will always be favored by those who feel that they must sacrifice an arm to loosen a neck from a noose.

Black rage exploded after the assassination of Dr. Martin Luther King in the spring of 1968. I remember watching the events on TV, in the dormitory lounge. Our reaction was shock initially, then anger, and then rage.

We channeled some of that rage into peaceful marches. I remember one march on Newport News. We stopped at a church along the way and "liberated" it. I don't know if the congregation realized that they had been liberated. The pastor was calling around trying to figure out how to keep these crazy college students in line. I wasn't one of the leaders of the movement. In fact, I was near the end of the line. I ended up in the balcony of the church, thinking, *This is not what this is supposed to be about,* but we liberated the church and had a rally and then continued on the march to Newport News.

In my junior year there was one demonstration that I wholeheartedly supported, though it called for a bit of sacrifice. At that time, many of the student leaders on campus were upset with the administration of Hampton and decided that we needed to take over the administration building in protest. We were not demonstrating for later curfews. We were demonstrating for student review boards of curriculum, later hours in the library. There were professors who, we felt, did not take our education seriously, and we wanted the opportunity to have some student input into the academic review process.

In a sense, the administration brought it upon itself. They had always told us how important and valuable education was, and we felt that we were not getting our fair share. They raised us to strive for excellence in education, and now we were holding their feet to the fire. But we considered ourselves a little more sophisticated and savvy with our demonstrations than with what we saw going on in the white campuses. We didn't destroy our building. We didn't hurt each other or anyone else, as a matter of fact. We wanted to do it in a very orderly, very dignified way, so when we took over the building, women slept upstairs and guys downstairs. Someone collected meal tickets, and food was brought in from the cafeteria. Some of the faculty members supported the demonstration and even sent in toothbrushes, toothpaste, and other toiletries.

I can remember calling home from the pay phone inside the administration building. Many of us were doing that. There were long lines behind the two phones that were there. My aunt and uncle wanted to come and get me and take me home. I said, "You can come, but I'm not coming out of here." They thought I was nuts. It was all the proof my aunt needed that I really was one of those radicals. My mother only said, "Don't do anything you'll be sorry for."

The Christians who were there banded together to write a letter to be read at the weekend IVCF retreat, a yearly, statewide retreat, to explain why we had chosen to demonstrate rather than be with them at the retreat. The letter explained that we believed that as Christians we had a responsibility to the other students to let them know that we cared about our education. We cared about standing with them on the things that were important to us as students. We reminded them that as Christians we really had the basis for the entire movement and that we couldn't pull up and go away while they were fighting for things that were important to all of us. We had to stand in the trenches. It was not time to go on retreats but advances.

Over the weekend, student leaders met with the Board of Trustees and we eventually resolved the issues. As a history major I was fascinated by the whole process. The whole time we were demonstrating I interviewed people and gathered documents and ended up writing my senior thesis on the campus event.

The season of my life spent in college also afforded me my first real contact and interaction with whites who felt that I was their equal. It was my first experience with "good whites." Many of those who taught me the basics of Christian life, the staff members of InterVarsity, were white. There were two women in particular who helped lay a foundation of faith in my life. Joyce was the embodiment of a gentle and quiet spirit. She was all kindness and compassion. When I fell, she would gently lift my spirit with words of encouragement and understanding. If Joyce was a living example of grace, then Beth could only be described as justice incarnate. She had a strong sense of right and wrong, good and bad, evil and truth. She didn't mince words. She let you know just what she thought of things, and if she worried that tact would somehow obscure the message of truth, then tact lost out. From Beth I learned the importance of standing up for my convictions no matter what the cost.

Elizabeth and Joyce earned my friendship. Most whites I encountered during college, both believers and nonbelievers, were willing to make an initial effort at friendship with a black person but were easily deterred if the offer wasn't immediately reciprocated. As soon as they sensed any rejection from the black community, they became angry that they weren't immediately accepted. They didn't seem to understand that at that point in history, most blacks had stored up a lifetime of memories of rejection and hatred from the white community. And as the saying goes, "once burned, twice wary." It's not surprising that many of us were skeptical at an initial show of friendship from a "honkey." We had to overcome years of distrust and anger to reach out and clasp an extended hand in our own. Sometimes that took time. But most white folks I encountered were impatient; they couldn't understand our reticence and quickly withdrew the hand they had extended.

For this reason, I really appreciated those who made an effort to consistently be amicable and show signs of wanting to develop a friendship. Beth and Joyce were rocks. I indulged myself in little mind games, pushing them to see how much indifference they were willing to tolerate in trying to win my trust. They took a lot. My heart warmed to them during this courtship, and eventually I reached out my hand to take theirs, and our fingers locked on one another.

I remember thinking that if I ever have a daughter, I want her to possess the characters of these two women. As I write this, I have a sixteen-year-old daughter named Elizabeth Joyce, who is well on her way to fulfilling that desire!

My career goal was to follow in the footsteps of those I admired most in life, the black educators at Webster Davis. I wanted to be a teacher. I set myself on that course the first semester of college and never wavered throughout my time there. That single-mindedness, combined with an impatience to get through school so that I could begin receiving a paycheck, propelled me to finish all my requirements by the end of my junior year. I know that a lot of students are convinced nowadays that college is a five year experience, but I was done in three. My grades reflected the fact that I should have stayed longer and concentrated more instead of trying to get the experience over with. I guess that is sort of an indication of how I attack life, particularly, difficult problems. Just get in, do it, and get it over with. In that same spirit I decided to use the first half of my senior year to fulfill my student-teaching requirement.

I had already decided that I wanted to be a teacher in an urban school. One of my teaching professors had told me that in the suburbs they were more interested in teaching the curriculum than they were in teaching the kids. Success was measured against two criteria: test scores and completing the curriculum on time.

"In urban areas," she said, her voice rising, "you will have much more opportunity to be creative. There success is measured by keeping the kids in the classroom, out of the halls, and off each other all day. Any learning that takes place is icing on the cake. Therefore, if you really enjoy teaching, if you really enjoy challenging the students, if you really want to be creative and care about kids, then the place to go is an urban school."

That was all the sales pitch I needed. Most of the student-teaching positions we heard about were for slots in rural and suburban areas near Hampton. There were a few openings in schools in the kind of neighborhood I grew up in, but I didn't consider that area urban enough. I wanted to break my teeth in a real city environment. Just as I was looking about, one of the boroughs in New York City came up with a program that was trying to get role models for the black students in the school system, so they decided to go south, to historically black colleges and universities, and recruit student teachers. I signed up without thinking twice.

Again, my family was shocked at what I was doing, but I think that they were beginning to expect such surprises from me. Aunt Pearl was scared to death for me because of all the stories she had heard about the rough neighborhoods of New York City. Mama was torn between pride and worry. My brothers wanted to get me a gun.

I left for my new home in Yonkers on a muggy day in September. It was the first time that I had spent any extended period of time out of the South. I remember thinking about how easy it was for us to keep our racism in order and remember whom we liked and didn't like in the South. But in the North it was much more complicated. Down here it was black and white. Up there it was everybody resenting and distrusting everybody else. It became ethnic and not just racial. It was the first time that I was really exposed to the Italian, the Irish, and the Asian communities, not to mention Puerto Ricans and Jamaicans. It was too complicated for me to figure out who didn't like whom and why.

Also, being raised a Southern black, I don't think that I was entirely prepared for what I saw in urban areas when I spent my time in Yonkers. I had my first taste of gangs, graffiti, violent fights, and students who defiantly cut class, cursed teachers, and didn't do homework. And Yonkers wasn't even known as one of the difficult school districts!

It was an interesting school because it sat right on the border between a very wealthy neighborhood and a very poor neighborhood. Probably the kids who created the most problems and were the most needy, were the kids I walked to school with every day. I stayed at an orphanage that housed a group of problem foster-care children whom no families would take in. The stories they told me about parents who neglected or abandoned them, drug-abusing mothers, violently abusive fathers, family members who sexually abused them and worse, made me appreciate my far-from-storybook childhood. The five months in Yonkers was a real growth experience, but it was enough to let me know that I didn't want to live in an urban environment and that I couldn't wait to get back home.

When I finished college in January, my intention was to find a job that would hold me over until the following school year began in September. I decided that I would try to find a teaching position somewhere in between comfortable Hampton, Virginia, and the challenge of New York City. I had actually had an interview with Richmond City Schools and had pretty good prospects for a job in September, but I needed something to keep me busy while all my friends finished their senior year.

A friend of mine who worked for the telephone company let me know that they were hiring. I jumped at the chance because it was difficult to find a company that would hire blacks, and AT&T in Virginia had a good reputation in black circles. So I reasoned that I could be an operator, and that would give me the ability to still be flexible with my time and go down to the college and see friends once in a while. I went in with the intention of applying for a job as an operator. They knew that I was a college graduate when they saw my transcripts. I must have interviewed well because they were puzzled as to why I was applying for an operator's slot. I almost didn't understand their question. I mumbled something like "I thought that's all I was qualified to do around here." The interviewer cut me off and suggested that I was qualified for a management position, and would I be interested? Again, I jumped. Within a week I was hired as a manager at C&P Telephone Company, then a part of AT&T. The unfortunate part of the story is that I never made it back to the classroom. Even today I regret that.

I found the office environment exhilarating. My co-workers didn't seem too shocked to be working with, and sometimes under, a black female. There were very few instances where my race or gender even cropped up as an issue. During the first two months I was there, just to show

how naive I was, my boss called me in and said, "Kay, you're doing a wonderful job. We're so excited to have you here. Do you have any friends who are looking for jobs right now?" I told him that most of my friends were still in school and wouldn't be finished until the summer. But then I thought of my friend, Helen Holbrook, who was moving to Richmond and might be interested in a position.

My boss's eyes lit up. "Well, good," he said, "let's have her come in. We can talk." So I brought Helen in, and she was interviewed, and she came out smiling. Then my boss asked me to step inside his office, and he closed the door behind me for privacy.

"She was real nice," he said rubbing his palms together, "but she's not exactly what we were looking for." And he hesitated. He couldn't quite figure out how to say it. When he had asked me if I had any friends looking for work, he meant black friends. The one I had sent was white. Color had never even crossed my mind.

I was amazed that a company was actually seeking out black college graduates. But that was the early seventies, and corporate America was waking up and realizing that there was an untapped pool of talent out there. Let's not say that they woke up on their own. A few thousand lawsuits helped open their eyes. In fact, many firms were trying to protect themselves from those lawsuits by aggressively trying to hire minorities. There was actually a run on black college grads for a few years. Corporate America was just beginning to open its doors . . . Well, in reality, not opening its doors—the doors were being blown off the hinges from the outside. It was not as if they invited us in out of the kindness and goodness of their heart. I was in the right place at the right time to be able to take advantage of that forced openness professionally.

Some of the experiences from those early years on the job shaped my views on the value of affirmative action and other aggressive recruitment of minorities. I saw many firms going out and hiring blacks for the sake of meeting their quotas and keeping the lawsuits from bankrupting their companies. That was during the period that they were hiring blacks to operate the elevators, answer phones, or do other mindless tasks just so they could count them as employees—the period when many of us had to fight to prove our competence because we had to prove to the more experienced managers that we were hired not just because we were black but also because we were capable of doing the job.

In retrospect, there was probably too much of a push by companies to "get them some Negroes" and put them in positions. Some were qualified and some were not. I had not been in the job very long before I was promoted and offered a transfer to Roanoke, Virginia, an area that we not so fondly referred to as the "sticks." One of the women in the office stopped by my cubicle and said in a voice that was obviously for my hearing, "I guess you have to be a Negro to go anywhere in this company today." I shot back at her without even thinking: "No, you just have to be good." But there was an element of truth in what she said at the time, and I resented it. I guess I spent a good portion of my professional career trying to prove that being black and being competent are not mutually exclusive.

I've added to that list since that time, to be black, female, pro-life, conservative and republican, and competent are not all mutually exclusive. I have been told that I was given the job because I was black. I have been told that I was given the job because I am a woman. I have been told that I was given the job to pay off pro-lifers. I have been told that I was given the job because I am a conservative "and they're trying to placate conservatives." That bothers me. It angers me because they miss the point that I can be all those things and entirely competent as well.

Determined to prove people like that woman wrong, I accepted the promotion and packed my bags for unknown territory. I spent my savings on a professional wardrobe, and after a quick good-bye to my family, I left for Roanoke about the time that most of my friends were graduating from college.

My time in college, the "radical years," was a phase to grow through, a healthy phase that left me with many needed insights into my identity as a black child of God. By the time we were seniors, we were much more tolerant of how others worked through their blackness. I came to understand that one's blackness is not determined by external things like hair styles or clothing. Nor does being poor or an underachiever make one "more black," as some in our culture would have us believe.

Celebrating one's heritage begins with a recognition that one is black, African-American, a person of color, a member of a minority community, however one wishes to describe oneself. The next step and, I feel, the crucial element in self-awareness for any person, is a knowledge of one's family history and a knowledge of the history of one's people. Such knowledge should be uncluttered by false scholarship that seeks to rewrite history with the goal of presenting any one race as either superior or inferior. We don't need any second-rate historians arguing that the Egyptians discovered things that they really didn't; we have enough cause for pride in the authentic story of our past. Storytellers like Alice Walker, James Baldwin, and Alex Haley have played a crucial role in inclining the hearts of black Americans to discover and celebrate their roots. My goal in this whole process is to develop an understanding of what has been, an appreciation of who we are, and a vision for who we can be in the future.

chapter nine
WORK AND MARRIAGE

P E R H A P S   A M B I T I O N wasn't the whole cause of my leaping at the transfer out of Richmond. My heart had been broken by a young man at Hampton who just couldn't seem to commit to a long-term relationship. At least not with me. I went to Roanoke with the intention of setting up a Protestant order of nuns. I was going to become a career woman. No men. No relationships. Both seemed to just get in the way. They used up too much mental energy and were just too much of a distraction.

My college roommate was from Roanoke, but she was leaving town just as I came in, and we only overlapped in that city by one day. But what a day it was! Before she left, Sharon did two things. She sold her car to me and introduced me to my future husband. Earlier in the day, Sharon just happened to run across this friend of hers and said, "Charles, why don't you come by? I want you to meet somebody tonight."

When Sharon told me that she had invited a "good buddy" of hers to meet me, I balked—"Don't even think what you're thinking." The last thing I needed, I thought, was a Cupid.

I met Charles that night. He disliked me immediately and I felt the same way about him. I don't think that two people ever had a worse first impression. It took me two seconds after seeing him amble in the door to classify him as a "Roanoke hick." He thought that I was a Richmond snob. He later made a comment to one of his friends that if it had rained that night, I would have surely drowned because my nose was so stuck up in the air. He was a motorcycle-riding, long-haired guy who hadn't finished college. He certainly wasn't the one I would've picked as a companion to walk with me through corporate America.

But before he even met me, Charles had promised Sharon that he would take me to dinner the following day. It would be my birthday and Sharon knew that I was going to be in town alone with no friends or acquaintances. She was feeling sorry for me and made Charles promise to take me out. Despite his immediate dislike for me, he kept his promise to Sharon.

So there we were the next night, gritting our teeth through what began as an extremely uncomfortable date. Then something happened. I noticed that although he hadn't finished school, Charles had a quick mind and had thought through a lot of the issues I was struggling with in my mind. The tide really began to turn when conversation turned to the subject of religion. I held my cards close to my chest to see where Charles stood. I discovered that the young man seated before me was the son, grandson, and great-grandson of Baptist preachers. *A good sign*, I thought.

But despite his heritage (or, perhaps, because of it), Charles' relationship to the church seemed like that of my uncle J.B. and aunt Pearl. He described what he thought was the illogical, emotion-laden element of the black Baptist church. He recalled times when he would question some of the simplistic interpretations his Sunday-school teachers and he would be quickly squelched. He told me about the women decked out in their finest who deliberately walked in late so that everyone could see them sashay down the aisle.

He told me about his baptism at age twelve.

"You see, the Baptists don't believe in baptizing babies, because they say babies aren't capable of making decisions about following Christ, so they wait until we're twelve and then tell us that 'You're a man now and you should join the church.' I didn't really believe any of the things that I confessed to believe, but I knew all the right things to say. And there was not a small bit of pressure to do so."

His words revealed ambivalent feelings towards the church and antipathy towards religion in general. Warning flags went up in my mind as I wondered just where Charles stood with the Lord. But a hopeful heart brushed aside worries. I reasoned to myself that he was disillusioned with his experience with Christianity but that he was surely a believer nonetheless. He had to be. I had never met anyone with such a thorough knowledge of the Bible and Christian history. Charles had received a scholarship to attend King College, a white Presbyterian college in eastern Tennessee. He was the brightest, most articulate man I had ever met who possessed an equally sharp sense of humor.

I found myself hoping that he would ask me out again. I wasn't disappointed. We were soon inseparable. He was the best friend I ever had. It didn't take long for us to realize that we were falling in love.

Inside I was torn. It had become clear enough through our time together that although Charles had grown up in the church and certainly knew more about the Bible than I, he did not have a personal relationship with God. I knew enough about the Bible to know that I was commanded not to be "yoked" with an unbeliever. Surely, that's where we were headed. So without any warning, one night when we were at a movie, I told Charles, "I'm becoming emotionally attached to you, and I don't want to do that because this relationship can never go anywhere. We have to stop seeing each other."

Charles never even stopped reaching for popcorn. "Okay," he agreed without a pause. But later he told me that he had been extremely disappointed. He took me home that night for what I thought was going to be our last time seeing each another. Tears welled up in my eyes before he even pulled up to my apartment. I was really going to miss him! Charles saw how upset I was and wanted to come in and sit with me until I calmed down. "No," I sniffed, "I have someone I can talk to."

He wondered who that "someone" was. And then he realized that I was talking about God. Who knows what raced through his mind at that moment? He told me later that for the first time in his life he understood that God was someone whom we could know and talk to, and even cry to, by ourselves. Soon Charles was crying, too. It comforted me to see that he was as distraught about our breaking up as I was. But his next comment let me know that it wasn't our break up that brought his tears.

"I want to know God like you do," he said. I offered to pray with him, and we held hands right there in my living room and prayed a simple prayer to ask Jesus to come into Charles's life. It was almost too simple for this biblical scholar. "That's it?" he asked. I assured him that it was, but I really wasn't as sure as I sounded. Was he just playing a game to keep our relationship going? I wanted to make sure that his conversion was for real, so I gathered up my courage and told him I thought that it would be best if we still didn't see each other for a while. He agreed that it would be best for us to separate and left.

I called him a few days later to talk about his conversion. "I don't feel any different," he said over the phone, "but I know that something's changed." I knew that something had changed when I saw him in church that Sunday. He didn't go through the service on automatic pilot as he used to. He looked genuinely interested when the pastor preached, and he followed along in his Bible. I dared to hope that perhaps Charles really had dedicated his life to the Lord.

He called me from time to time to fill me in on what he was learning. His enthusiasm seeped out of the phone. "I *am* a new creature!" he exulted. And he was. Gone was the cynicism and bookish interest in the Bible. Taking its place was a thirst for knowledge and spiritual growth. We started spending time together again. In two months he asked me to marry him.

We were in my apartment, reading the comics, when a strange look came across Charles's face. "Kay, will you marry me?" he asked. Just like that. No warning. No candlelit dinner at a fancy restaurant. And I said yes. Just like that. No hesitation. Our wedding was scheduled for three months later, the only weekend that my friends Doug Holladay and Skip Ryan were both going to be in Richmond.

I was an absolute snit about my wedding. I hadn't completely left the natural phase I entered during my college years. Flowers, dresses, make-up, rings, and decorations all held little interest for me. I pretty much told my aunt and my bridesmaids that they could handle all those details and just let me know what time I needed to show up. If I had understood more of what marriage is like and the commitment that I was making, I know that I would have been more enthused.

Charles and I drove to Richmond on a Wednesday and were married that Saturday. It was a simple ceremony. We didn't have much money for a honeymoon so we thought we ought to go somewhere relatively cheap. Charles suggested Manhattan. Where did we get the idea that New York City was cheap? We couldn't even afford a room-service breakfast at our hotel. But both of us really enjoy theater, and so the thought of attending a Broadway play sounded regal. On the flight up, we listed all the museums and parks that we wanted to visit.

What we *didn't* know was how cold it can get in New York in January. It was freezing. Walking to the theater district was out of the question and we hadn't planned on the expense of taxis, so we pretty much stayed in our hotel room the whole time. No plays, no museums, no walks in the park. Just the two of us in our cozy little hotel room. Like I said, Charles is pretty smart.

On the way back to Roanoke we stopped in Richmond

to pick up our wedding gifts, and with our car packed to the ceiling with toasters and blenders, we headed home.

One of the first things we did once we settled in was try to find a church that we both liked. We tried many black churches and loved the music and fellowship with other black Christians. In so many ways, we felt right at home, but both of us had a strong hunger for more biblical teaching and solid theology and less "preaching and entertainment."

Then I remembered that when I had moved to the area, some friends from IVCF told me to contact the Inter Varsity Christian Fellowship (IVCF) representative in Roanoke. He turned out to be Reverend Jack Arnold, the pastor of a Presbyterian church in the white section of town. We had a nice chat on the phone and he invited me to Grace Church. Of course I didn't go.

When it became clear, however, that we weren't going to find what we were looking for in the black churches in Roanoke at that time, Charles and I dropped by Grace Church one Sunday. We loved the service. It had everything we were looking for: a theology that recognized the sovereignty of God, a pastor who encouraged personal spiritual growth, and an active evangelistic outreach. It had everything we wanted in a church—except black folks. And that was a major obstacle. This was 1974, and although the rest of the nation was getting used to the idea of integration, most churches were still segregated. Maybe not officially, but certainly in practice. While we liked Grace Church, it was unthinkable that we would become members there. But we did.

On our first visit we provoked many stares and whispers. Our second time, we were the talk of the whole congregation. The pastor greeted us warmly at the door and introduced us to a few members of the congregation who, after an initial bout of shock, welcomed us. It became clear that the church was willing to try integration if we were. Were we?

Charles had jarred his family already by announcing that at age twenty-two he had become a Christian. "No, no, you're just rededicating your life," they told him. "No, I have just been born-again. I have accepted Christ as my Savior for the first time in my life. I am *now* a Christian." They would just shake their heads and murmur about how going to that white school had sure messed him up. "You've been in church all your life, you've been baptized, and now you're talking about 'becoming a Christian?!'" It was beyond their understanding. How would they handle Charles's and my choosing to attend a white church?

As we expected, they took our going to Grace Church as a slap in the face. As much as we tried to smooth things over, there were hurt feelings. It was not the last time that we would choose spiritual growth over comfort.

Once the church leadership recognized Charles's biblical knowledge, which now was combined with solid faith, they elected and ordained him as a deacon. Charles said once that in his earlier years he had never been able to build a spiritual foundation because all he had were "bricks" of biblical knowledge. Without Christ, they were just a useless pile. It wasn't until he became a believer that he had the "mortar" that he needed to build a solid foundation.

Our time at Grace was not without racial slights. I became involved in a women's Bible study that met once a week for learning and fellowship. One of the highlights of the year was a trip to Myrtle Beach with the families of the women in our study. All year long, references to the annual family beach trip were dropped into conversation. I had heard so many stories about the fun times they had together that I was really looking forward to going. But we were never invited. As summer drew near, I overheard women making arrangements for shared beach houses, but the conversation would die down whenever I came near. The group left for the beach without us, and I was crushed. I'd never felt so betrayed and rejected.

Eventually embarrassment and hurt died down enough for me to ask one day in Bible study why Charles and I weren't included in the beach trip. An uncomfortable silence fell upon the room. "Well, Kay, we just felt that—well you

know that there aren't very many black people at Myrtle
Beach . . . and we just thought you would be uncomfortable." They were concerned for *us*? Didn't they see the
irony? It took all my courage to read our Scripture verse out
loud before the group, but I wanted to say something else. I
did. "I guess I thought that if we wouldn't be accepted at a
certain vacation spot, that you would choose another one
rather than leave us out." Nothing more was ever said about
it.

• • •

When I met him, Charles was two courses shy of his
college degree and working as a mail clerk for a correspond-
ence school. C&P was still in its black-hiring frenzy and he
soon came to work for Ma Bell on the technical end of
business while I supervised operators in a separate building.
He traveled much more than I did, which made finishing
those last two courses a challenge, but we worked out a
system where I registered for those classes and attended
school with him, and was there to take notes when he had
to travel. I'll never forget how amused the folks at the
telephone company were when they found out that he had
received his degree. I don't think that they ever realized that
he *didn't* have one.

When I moved from Richmond, which I considered a
big city, to Roanoke, which I considered the sticks, I
anticipated many more problems as a black, female manager. Actually, little Roanoke proved to be much more
progressive and accepting than cosmopolitan Richmond. In
fact, it was the management team in Roanoke who re-
quested that I be transferred there. Early on in my time with
the phone company, when I was still in Richmond, the
company had a state-wide strike. All management employees were sent to various parts of the state to work the switch
boards and other union jobs. I was sent to Roanoke. I
remember crossing the picket line. The picketers would
leave the management types alone, knowing that this was

expected in a strike, but they kept calling me a "scab" and yelling awful names at me. They had never seen a black in management before and thought that I was a strike breaker.

Then the word began to pass among the employees in line that I was a manager. The black employees on strike became so excited that there was a black manager that they not only left me alone, but some would cheer as I entered the building. When the strike was over, several of the employees told me how proud they were of me.

I met several of the managers from Roanoke during the strike and as a result, when they were trying to break down some of the racial barriers in the management ranks there, they called to Richmond to see if I could be transferred to Roanoke. It was a good move for me because I had the support of the management team as well as the union people, who were thrilled to see a black person in management. I've often wondered what made the folks in Roanoke so much more accepting of a black manager. Perhaps it has something to do with the dynamics of a small city.

It was during those next few years that I really learned how to manage people. C&P and AT&T offered excellent training courses for their young managers. I learned how people learn; how to supervise people; how to make decisions. They trained us well. Many of the more senior managers took a special interest in me because they were dedicated to my success as one of the first black managers. They wanted to give me all the tools that I could use. I still use the skills I learned from those courses.

Two of the principles I learned are the importance of a sense of humor and the power of not losing your cool. Once, when I supervised the Directory Assistance office, one of the black operators received an obnoxious caller who threatened, "Listen, you better give me that number!" She tried very hard to find the number but couldn't. He demanded to speak to her supervisor, so she put me on the line, warning me that this was a live one.

"Can I help you, sir?" I asked in my sweetest voice. A gruff voice on the other end barked at me, "Can you get me that number? That stupid nigger wouldn't give me the number." I said, "Well, sir, this one can't either because the number is not published." He hung up.

Another time, we had a flurry of calls. We had to put everyone on the boards to answer the calls so I was pulling people off breaks and gathering as many as I could to handle the load. I pulled one of the service assistants, a white woman a decade or so my senior, off her assignment and put her at the boards. The flood lasted about twenty minutes and then died down, so I began to take some of them off.

"Gee, Kay," the woman said, taking off her head set. "What was that? I was sweating like a nigger!" I looked her square in the eye and said, "I more than anyone know *exactly* what you mean!" When she realized what she had said, she was in shock, horrified at what had slipped out of her mouth. I could have disciplined her, but in this case a humorous retort taught her more than a get tough approach.

My life as a career woman was taking off. I became a supervisor of a larger directory assistance office. Then I moved across the hall to become a force manager for long distance. My job entailed forecasting the number of employees needed to handle the estimated volume of calls while providing maximum service and efficiency to customers. It was like a game. We would look at data from last year, last week, last month, and then make decisions about how many people we needed for every fifteen-minute period. It was scheduled that closely. The trick was never paying too many people to sit around during slack times, but always having enough to provide quality service. I was really enjoying work. Charles and I had discussed starting a family, and we even stopped using birth control for a short period. But then there was talk of giving me another promotion, and we decided to put off having children until I had plateaued at work. But it was too late. I was pregnant.

We had already made the decision that when we had children, one of us would stay home with them. We had talked with other young black couples about the trends we saw with the black family. Somebody had to be giving full attention to the children.

We actually had a conversation about whether the one staying home would be Charles or me. In retrospect I can't believe that we even entertained the thought that he would come home. Charles just does not have the temperament to be a full-time child rearer. There may be a few men out there who are, but not most. Charles was not the nurturer. He didn't have the nesting instincts. He also didn't have the ability to nurse. So we made the decision that I would come home.

Leaving the power and prestige of my office job was made easier by the fact that I was sick as a dog my first four months of pregnancy. It didn't take long before I couldn't wait to stop working. My co-workers at the office threw a huge baby shower. They were so generous that Charles and I literally had everything we needed for the baby and did not have to buy anything until well into the first year.

In June of 1974, Charles Everett James, Jr. came into the world with a shriek, and he continued to cry for about nine months straight. I had a very colicky child. He was a screaming little bundle of raw nerves. He was a clutchy, clinging baby who would cry if I went out of his sight. Charles was such a demanding baby that I really couldn't enjoy the benefits of being home and raising a baby. A dark cloud hovered. It may have been postpartum depression, it may have been exhaustion. Chuck, as we called Charles Jr., never slept more than a couple of hours at night. When he awakened, he screamed. Both Charles and I were physically worn out.

Because Chuck couldn't stay in the nursery, I couldn't go to church. We tried to go to Charles's office picnic that summer, but I had to leave early because Chuck's screams were setting everybody on edge. Just going to the grocery store was an ordeal. Eventually a compassion squad from the church came to rescue us. A few women would take turns spending the night with us, getting up to take care of

Chuck so that Charles and I could get some sleep. Poor Charles, I was almost as needy as Chuck. He ended up taking care of me and the baby to some extent. From day one, I never had to ask him to change a diaper or feed one of the children or give a bath. There may be difficult issues in our marriage, but that's never been one of them.

People I knew, especially Christians, kept telling me that this was a wonderful, noble calling. I could not figure it out. All I knew was that my house was a wreck. I was exhausted all the time. We didn't have any money. We had gone from two people on two good incomes to three on one. To make matters worse, my petite frame never lost the pounds I had gained in pregnancy. I ended up wearing all of Charles's clothes because I couldn't afford to buy new ones. I went from wearing business suits to my husband's jeans.

At the same time, Charles's career with C&P was taking off. While I couldn't get it together at home, he was coming home telling me about his business lunches and all the neat places he had been. He was running in, packing his bags, and kissing me on the cheek as he ran out the door saying he was going to be gone for two days on a business trip. I grew resentful and angry. But at least I saw a light at the end of the tunnel. When he turned nine months old, Chuck began to quiet down a little.

And then it happened. I had learned to be meticulous about birth control but I couldn't take birth control pills because I became violently ill. When I was on the pill, I felt pregnant all the time, not a good feeling. So we began to use condoms and spermicide as a method of birth control. Like they say, this is not a one-hundred-percent effective method of birth control. We know. As soon as Charles suspected the condom had torn, he got down on his knees and prayed, "Lord, please let this not happen. Please, Lord, don't let Kay be pregnant."

While waiting for the results of the pregnancy test, I went shopping with Sharon, the friend who had introduced me to Charles. We were in the grocery store—the produce section to be exact—when it was time to call the doctor's office. "Congratulations, Mrs. James," the voice said, "you're pregnant." As upset as I had been up until that point, as soon as it became clear that I was going to have another child, I felt a certain peace. Charles and I had done everything possible (except abstinence) to prevent a pregnancy and if despite our best efforts I was still pregnant, then I knew that it was God's will for us to have another child. For my husband and me, the result of a condom breaking was my only daughter—Elizabeth—the sunshine of my life. Three years later, the same thing happened, and I became pregnant with my pride and joy, Robbie, our third child.

I reveal the intimate details of this story for a reason. Years later when I was Assistant Secretary for Public Affairs at the U.S. Department of Health and Human Services, the issue of condoms came up as the government struggled with a response to the epidemic of AIDS and other sexually transmitted diseases. I was vehemently opposed to the government's promoting what was slickly named "safe sex." Reporters were constantly prodding me about my stance, wanting to know if it was my Christian conservative ideology that compelled me to oppose the "safe sex" campaign. Finally, a reporter from the *Washington Post* called me one Saturday morning at home. The car was packed, Charles and the kids were in the car waiting for me, and the reporter wanted to know my ideological reasons for opposing condom distribution to teens. "Let me tell you something off-the-record," I confided. "I have two condom kids. The result of condom failure for my husband and me has been two wonderful kids whom we adore and treasure. The result for someone else could be death."

I knew firsthand of the imperfect record of condoms in preventing pregnancy. Even Planned Parenthood concedes that condoms fail 15.7 percent of the time over the course of a year. This means that the chances of getting pregnant though faithfully using a condom are one in six. Those odds are under the best of circumstances, when condoms are used for their intended purpose, to prevent pregnancy during vaginal intercourse.

It is much easier, however, to contract HIV (human immunodeficiency virus) than to become pregnant. You can only get pregnant several days out of a month; you can catch HIV every day and night of the year. In addition, viruses are one of the smallest living organisms known to man, hundreds of times smaller than a sperm cell. That means that it is much easier and much more likely for a virus to slip through small pores or tears in latex condoms.

The truth is, we really don't know how effective condoms are in preventing the spread of sexually transmitted diseases such as AIDS. However, laboratory tests conducted by the University of California at Los Angeles show that condoms fail to prevent the passage of HIV *between one in four and one in ten times* depending upon the brand. And remember, these tests were done in a stationary test tube, with no motion or friction to break down the latex or propel the virus.

In fact, in 1988, the Department of Health and Human Services had to cut off funding for a large-scale trial of the effectiveness of condoms in preventing the spread of HIV, specifically in anal sex, because of concerns that condoms were incapable of providing reliable protection for the study's participants. A high rate of HIV infection among the male homosexual population combined with the risks of condom use translated into the probability of significant numbers of men in the study contracting HIV.

Even former Surgeon General C. Everett Koop, a highly visible advocate of condom use to prevent the spread of AIDS, had to revise his overly optimistic analysis of the protective value of condoms. In his words, prophylactics have "extraordinarily high" failure rates among homosexuals and offer them no assurance of "safe sex." Despite these facts, the U.S. government has launched a campaign to convince our sexually active population, particularly homosexuals, that they can have "safe sex" if they faithfully use condoms. I entered into the fray when the Department wanted to publish a graphic brochure touting "safe sex" and the value of condoms in preventing HIV infection. The brochure gave the required lip service to abstinence, saying that it is the only one-hundred-percent effective protection against AIDS, and then without so much as a period to give one cause to ponder, it went on to say, "but used properly, condoms can reduce the risk of sexually transmitted diseases (STDs) such as HIV."

The unspoken message is that since no one is going to choose abstinence and sexual intercourse with one mutually faithful partner (in the old days we called that being a virgin until marriage and then staying faithful to your spouse), then here's your best option:

"Condoms reduce the risk of acquiring STDs like AIDS." Reduce the risk? *AIDS is fatal.* Is this the best we can do for our children? How much do condoms reduce the risk of catching a disease that will make tumors grow on their skin, make fungus grow on their tongue and throat, and turn them into living skeletons? "Safe sex?" Please, let's at least be honest with the people and tell them the best a condom will provide is "saf*er* sex." In the words of Gary Bauer, president of the Family Research Council, "Using a condom to protect against HIV is like playing Russian Roulette." In my mind, it makes sense to advocate the highly unreliable protection afforded by condoms only to those people unwilling to abstain from high-risk sexual intercourse.

Before I leave the subject of sex and America's youth, I need to set the record straight. Our nation's young people are not the lustful, hormone-driven, no-brainers that many would have us believe. Although teen sexual activity rates are rising (more steeply in the white community than in the black community), we should not accept teenage sex as a given. When presented with virginity as a positive life choice, along with the facts on pregnancy, HIV, gonorrhea, syphilis, and the other consequences of sexual activity, many choose abstinence. In fact, half of eighteen-year-olds have never had premarital sex. And many teenagers who

have experienced intercourse are choosing "second virginity."

A Louis Harris poll showed that ninety percent of teens
admitted having become sexually active simply because of
perceived peer pressure. Eighty percent said that they felt
that they had been drawn into it too soon. Is teenage sex
inevitable? I'd say not. But handing out condoms in school
only reinforces the message that "everyone is doing it" and
so should you. Those who consider teaching abstinence
"unrealistic" should consider the impressive results of
abstinence based sex education curricula.

The timing of my becoming pregnant with Elizabeth
was not good. Physically I was weak, and emotionally I was
a wreck. Still, I learned a valuable lesson from that experience which helped years later when history repeated itself.
That is, *an unwanted pregnancy is not an unwanted child.* All
three of my pregnancies have been mistimed and un-
planned, and yet all three of my children have been
cherished additions to the family.

The second lesson I learned was that to pull through,
women in crisis pregnancies need the help and support of
their family and community. I really needed the folks from
our church to come over and have an adult conversation
with me, to watch Chuck one morning a week so that I
could run errands, to pass along baby clothes.

And I needed help with mothering skills. Although I
came from a large family, I had been raised essentially as an
only child by my aunt and uncle. My education had
prepared me to be a high-school history teacher, so I knew
something about adolescence, but I had absolutely no idea
what to do with a baby or toddler. I needed help learning
how to nurse, how to discipline, how to care for a sick baby.
Fortunately, there was an older woman in our congregation
at Grace Church with a vision for teaching young mothers.
Her name is Phil Brokaw, and she had a ministry that I hope
one day in her honor I can duplicate. She would invite
younger women on Wednesday mornings to her house. We
dropped off the babies at the church nursery and drove to

her home where we would attend a Bible study and training time on parenting and marriage relationships. I looked forward to those three hours all week! It was such a treat to dress up and eat a meal of adult food that had been prepared for us and to sit and have uninterrupted conversations with other young mothers.

The other godsend during that difficult period was a book that Beth York suggested I read: *What Is a Family?* by Edith Schaffer, which gives a motivating and encouraging depiction of what family life can and should be. She painted a word picture in my mind of a healthy family and home life. I learned how a family is supposed to function and some practical advice for making that happen. As I read, I was energized about my life at home with the kids. It was as if someone had turned on a light switch after two years of darkness. Growing up in a dysfunctional family, I had never really seen motherly and fatherly affection and guidance modeled. Her book gave me a vision.

Then I became super-mom. You could almost hear the Rocky music in the background as I cleaned the house. I was baking homemade bread and making my own peanut butter. I never again bought commercial baby food; I made my own with a baby-food grinder. I began "creating memories" for the kids. Edith Schaffer talked about how very often in twentieth-century living we want to give our children things instead of *memories*. Memories they can keep forever, while things wear out. It was more important to take the kids on a really fun picnic and show them something special than it was to buy them a new toy that would be gone in six months if it lasted that long. So I took them on nature walks, and went to museums, and took them to concerts and spent time talking with them, sharing stories that my mother had shared with me. I realized the importance of putting fresh flowers on the table and creating a comforting environment in the home.

One Wednesday morning at the young mothers' Bible study, one of the women spoke about her involvement with a crisis pregnancy center called *Birthright*. She let us know that they needed volunteers. She said to me later (as I was one of a few black mothers in the Bible study) that a number of the women who called in were black and that it would be very nice to have some black counselors who could make these young women feel more comfortable. I came home not knowing for certain how Charles felt about abortion because we had never had a conversation about it. I was very proud of myself for volunteering to work at *Birthright*, and I hoped that he would be proud of me, too. And he was. He felt even more passionately about the need for black mothers like me to volunteer at crisis pregnancy centers than I did.

So with Charles's blessing, I would pack up Chuck a few days a week and take him with me to the *Birthright* center to answer phones or stuff envelopes in between calls. That was my first exposure to the issue. I was horrified at what I learned and saw. I knew instinctively that killing an unborn baby was wrong, but I had never studied it as an issue. When I began to read the literature and see the pictures and as I became more educated about the issue, I felt very deeply about it. Something akin to righteous indignation stirred within.

I continued my volunteer work at *Birthright* until the call we had been waiting for came through, and Charles was promoted to Richmond.

chapter ten
MELTED BUTTER AND HARDENED CLAY

T I M E A W A Y F R O M A P R O B L E M often has the
effect of backing you away from a mountain you're trying to
climb. The distance gives you perspective on the overall size
of the mountain, and allows you to plot a course over its
easier terrain. Our years in Roanoke were the distance that I
needed to gain perspective on the relationships in my life
that needed mending and the people who needed help.
Upon returning to Richmond, I realized how sick and in
need of help my father was.

My mother moved in with us and she spent her day
cleaning our house until the floors shone. Charles and the
kids weren't used to kitchen floors that didn't stick, and
ironed socks, but they soon adjusted. Her help gave me a lot
more free time. Determined not to let that free time get
sponged up by the afternoon soaps, I set out on my first
project: to help my father receive help for his alcoholism.

First, I needed to find him. He and my mother had
stopped speaking years before, but in recent years he had
cut off almost all contact with his kids as well. He had
remarried and lived somewhere on the east side of town.
One day one of my brothers ran into him at a car dealership

where he worked as a janitor. I tracked him down. I had checked into all the drug and alcohol treatment centers available. There wasn't much, and what was available was incredibly expensive.

Unfortunately, one of my brothers was following right in my father's footsteps. Lucky, one of the middle children, had become the type of alcoholic that drank Irish Rose out of a dirty paper sack as he sat on park benches with his friends. I would drive around at night, poking through alleys and parks, looking for him among the odd assortment of red-eyed homeless men. I'd put the kids in the front of the car with me and drag an inebriated Lucky into the back seat where he'd stretch out and sleep. At home we'd let him shower and shave and fix himself up, and he'd leave the house the next morning, promising that he wouldn't touch any alcohol that day. He was going to look for a job. And then every night I'd search the parks and alleys for him to bring him home again.

I continued these search-and-rescue missions for my brother and father for about six months before my heart grew sick. It wasn't the string of lies and broken promises that disheartened me; it was the trauma of having to see them in such a low state, day after day. It hurt me to see two men whom I loved so dearly slowly killing themselves with alcohol. I just backed off entirely. Eventually, Lucky responded to treatment and has been clean and sober for more than ten years. My father's alcoholism eventually killed him.

When I finally acknowledged to myself that there was little more I could do for my father, I began to look around for part-time volunteer work. I was looking for something that would empower the black community. Charles and I became testers with a fair-housing project. We would go in and try to buy or rent property to see if we were being discriminated against as blacks. Boy, did that experience ever open my eyes! It was not the typical confederate-flag-waving Southerner that surprised us. We already knew that his type didn't like our type, and we expected to be stonewalled whenever we tried to move into "Bubba"

-dominated neighborhoods. What surprised us was the subtle discrimination from those who lead you to be believe that they are progressive on the race issue.

For example, I can remember one assignment I went on that I thought was a complete waste of time because I had black friends who lived in the particular apartment complex that we were testing. I went into the rental office, dressed like the picture of a Richmond Junior Leaguer. By all outward appearances I was lighter skinned than the woman behind the counter, who was very friendly and made idle chitchat as she searched her paperwork to see if they had any two-bedroom apartments available. She asked me where I had bought my skirt and then asked me where we lived now, and I told her we lived on the south side.

"Ah, that's God's country," she sighed. "I love it over there." "Yeah," I nodded. "But God doesn't have to take the bridge over to work every morning. That's why we want to live over here." It was a warm, pleasant exchange, and she looked genuinely sad as she told me that there were no openings at the time. "Why don't you check back after the end of the month?" She added as I left, "We often have more openings then." She said that she couldn't promise anything but would be happy to take our application.

As I walked back to the car, I saw a couple of little black kids building sand castles in the playground sandbox. *No discrimination here*, I thought. When I reached the car around the corner, I didn't say anything and let the white tester go in. It grew hot and humid sitting in the car. I couldn't imagine what was taking him so long. It only took me about ten minutes to get my answer. When he strolled out thirty minutes later and got in the car, I asked, "Bruce, what took you so long? I've been melting in this car!"

"I don't know how you got through those two empty apartments so fast," he replied. I stared at him blankly. "You have to be kidding," I said testily. "No . . . Didn't she show them to you?" That's when I realized two things about race in America. First, despite laws and much progress, racism still exists in America. It's just more insidious because it's gone underground. The second thing I realized is that quotas are no easy answer. That woman felt safe in turning me away because she had her quota of blacks in the complex, and she wasn't accepting any more. She could discriminate against me and probably win any lawsuit we tried to bring because she could prove she had some blacks in there. That's when I began to question quotas. I began to see them as a sort of glass ceiling that one couldn't rise above. It was actually protecting these people who were discriminating against me.

That scenario was repeated over and over again during the time that Charles and I were testers. I use that experience to explain to black college students or young professionals that you can have the clothes, you can have the car, you can have all of the outside trappings, but you're still black. All it took to be denied an apartment was my skin color.

Another favorite technique of those in the real estate business to keep their neighborhoods color free is "steering." It happened to us recently when we looked for a house after our move to Washington, D.C. We drove out to a housing development where they were building new homes. The developer, a friendly guy in jeans and a blazer, said that all the lots had been sold and that they were about to close out the development. He gave us a tip, though, that down the street and across the way there was an older development with better prices. Even after being a fair-housing tester, Charles and I didn't think anything of it. We thanked him and headed out to the neighborhood he had mentioned. It wasn't until we noticed a little black child on a tricycle and a black man going out to get his mail that we realized we had been steered.

Once when I spoke to the Board of Realtors in Richmond, I started out by saying: "My husband plays golf. My daughter takes ballet lessons at the Richmond ballet. My son plays soccer. We teach Sunday school, take vacations at the beach, yet I can't live in your neighborhood." If it can happen to me, imagine what is happening to the over-whelming majority of black citizens in this country.

I think that sometimes discrimination is so subtle that not even the bigots realize what motivates their feelings. Many times when I was with the phone company and then later when I worked in personnel with an electronics chain, I would talk with my co-workers about a job candidate whom they had rejected. What was it about him or her you didn't like? I'd ask, because the applicants were very qualified for the position. The response I'd get was a vague, "I can't put my finger on it, but I just don't think that he or she would be right for the job."

Charged up by experiences like the one at that apart-ment building, Charles and I continued to volunteer with Housing Opportunities Made Equal (HOME). Once Robbie, our youngest child, was in school, I worked full-time and went on paid staff. My first role was to supervise the testing program, something I felt very comfortable doing. My second assignment was more of a stretch. At the encourage-ment of Barbara Wurtzel, the Executive Director of HOME, I was put in charge of a year-long community outreach program. It was my first involvement with television and the media, and I felt overwhelmed and intimidated. It amazed me when friends or family would see me run a press conference or speak out against housing discrimina-tion on TV and say that they felt that I am truly gifted in public speaking and working the press. I continually felt incompetent and in over my head.

I was flattered and somewhat relieved when Barbara's husband, Alan, who was chairman of the board of Circuit City, a chain of electronics stores, invited me to work there in human resources. I left HOME for the corporate world. We both thought that it would be great experience, and with three kids we really needed the money.

•   •   •

When we left Grace Church in Roanoke, many in the congregation suggested that we try Stoneypoint, a sister

Presbyterian church in Richmond. We did, hoping to find at least a handful of black families in the congregation. There were none, but we couldn't walk away from the teaching, fellowship, and evangelism that we found there. We decided to integrate the Presbyterians again.

Our choosing Stony Point proved providential. It was there that we met Pat Soehl, a young man fired up about the issue of abortion. Pat was really concerned because he felt that the Protestant Christian community in Richmond had not stepped up to the issue of abortion. He felt that we tended to be judgmental, while the Catholic Church tended to be more involved in the mercy ministries. We would wave the proverbial finger in the face saying, "You should not have an abortion," but we weren't providing alternatives for women.

What he really meant was that we didn't have many organized efforts to aid women in crisis pregnancies. The truth is that individuals and families have for centuries assisted neighbors and kin caught in crisis pregnancies. The black community has an especially rich history of caring for its mothers in need. I am a perfect example of that helping tradition. My aunt and uncle stepped in to help my mother when she desperately needed help raising her kids. But Pat was concerned that the need had reached such a level and the abortion rate was climbing so drastically that we really needed to expand and institutionalize our efforts.

A small group of believers came together and began praying about what sort of help we could provide to complement the efforts of the Catholic Church and other charities. We set up a steering committee, which performed a lot of the legwork, needs analysis, and proposal writing. We also invited Kurt Young, who at that time was executive director of the Christian Action Council, to meet with our steering committee and offer counsel. He came in and helped us with the details and logistics of actually setting up a crisis pregnancy center. The next step was establishing a board of directors. I served on the first board. The pastor of my church volunteered to chair the board, and someone in the congregation did the legal work to get the center incorporated. Charles and I used the goodwill of all of our friends and associates to get the CPC off the ground, a skill that we have honed through the years.

That first board dealt with issues such as location. We didn't want the center to be located in the suburbs; we wanted it accessible to poor women. Still, we wanted it to be in a neighborhood where volunteers would feel comfortable coming and going.

From the beginning we tried to make the center a biracial endeavor that would serve black and white women. From the very onset, however, many more whites than blacks were involved in the center. Some of the white volunteers asked me why black Christians weren't more interested in assisting women in crisis pregnancies. I've since learned that that sort of exchange is very typical of the black/white experience. We had to set up a formal organization to do what the black church was doing anyway. It wasn't that black Christians weren't interested. In fact, many of the black pastors whom we called and talked to about working with a Crisis Pregnancy Center had dealt with five cases that week. Their response was typically, "What do you mean? We *are* a crisis pregnancy center."

Exactly the same thing happened when the white evangelical community awoke to the need for adoption services. All the surveys they conducted showed that black families are much less likely than white families to formally adopt children. But those surveys didn't take into account the fact that *black churches and black families have practiced informal adoption for generations.* (I'm a perfect example of that). The reality is, if you go before a black audience and ask, "How many of you were raised by a grandmother, aunt, uncle, brother, sister, godmother, neighbor, or someone other than your parents?" you are going to see a lot of hands go up. In most of these cases there were never any court papers signed, no one ever appeared before a judge, no home visits were made, and no one ever launched a public awareness campaign to tell us that these children needed to be taken into someone's home. It was just a matter of the community's pulling together and doing what needed to be done.

It was interesting to me as I observed the "pro-life"/"pro-choice" debate evolving—that while the people on the other side of the debate called themselves "pro-choice," they weren't providing choices for women. Very often as I talked with young women at the Crisis Pregnancy Center, they would say, "I'm having this abortion because I feel like I have no choice." In most cases, they were telling the truth. They *had* no choice. The boyfriend had left, offering no support. Many girls were afraid to let their parents know that they were pregnant, so abortion seemed the only viable option. In many cases, it was a single parent with one or two children, and she saw no hope of being able to manage yet another child. Choice seemed a strange concept to these women.

I discovered that as one sat down with each individual woman and worked through her particular situation—provided her with some alternatives so that she had an option other than abortion—the overwhelming majority of them would choose life. And so I thought, and still believe today, that a better use of our time for individuals on both sides of the abortion debate is to provide support services and options for women so that they don't have to make that choice. Everyone agrees that "Oh, it's a difficult choice, it's a heart-wrenching choice, it's a choice I wish I didn't have to make." So why not invest our time and energy in providing options so that no woman ever has to make that choice?

I don't think there's anything better that we can do with our time than to provide options for a woman so that she doesn't have to take the life of her unborn child. There are not many volunteer experiences where you know for certain that when you give your time and energy, you are literally saving lives. Not only do volunteers save the life of an unborn child but they prevent the psychological torment that a woman would have to go through when she's powerless and without options. Providing options and saving lives—what higher calling can we have?

The services we offered women included finding housing among sympathetic families in the Christian community. We also helped mothers to "access the system." It amazed me how often women felt like they had no choice because they didn't know of the support services available to them. I think very often that middle-class women, and women who know how to work the system, take it for granted that others know what services are available to them. We found that there were many services that went unused just for lack of understanding. We lead women through the labyrinth of bureaucracy, paperwork, and lines to receive food stamps, Medicaid, and public assistance. Some folks might think it's strange that a conservative like me spent many years helping folks to get on welfare, but that's exactly what welfare was intended to be: a safety net. Welfare needs to be available for women in situations like a crisis pregnancy. But alongside public assistance needs to be the life plan to move on beyond dependency. Counselors would work with women to set career or educational goals, to set priorities and life goals, so that welfare does not become a way of life.

We also provided the very practical needs such as cribs, car seats, and baby clothes. We offered classes on childbirth and parenting. State-of-the-art clinics now offer services such as establishing paternity, legal advice on child support and job training. Last but not least, we offered friends and a support system for a woman who was going through a crisis in her life. For many women, the most helpful service that we provided was a number to call and a friend to talk to during a very difficult time. We held a press conference on our opening day to let the media and the public know that we were there to offer alternatives to women in need.

Because I had three young children of my own at that point, my volunteer activity was limited to my role on the Board. But Charles and I had our name on the list of supporters and were often called upon to open our home to

a pregnant woman, or a woman and her baby. We had
several women come live with us. Sometimes it was a young
pregnant girl who needed somewhere to live; other times it
was a new mother and her baby. I huffed and blew my way
through several deliveries as a Lamaze coach.

It was during this time that I was also forced to come to
terms with my relationship with my aunt and uncle. J.B.
went into the hospital for some fairly routine surgery and
died when a blood clot broke loose. A nurse found him dead
in his bed. I was angry at him for leaving. He had been a
loving and stable force in an otherwise turbulent childhood.
A few bitter feelings lingered about his not standing up for
me, but as I matured and as I learned more about the
disease of alcoholism, I realized that withdrawal and
nonconfrontation was his way of dealing with my aunt.
Growing up, I despised him for his weakness and submis-
siveness to her, but I came to understand that his behavior
was not motivated by a lack of love for me. He adopted the
demeanor that he needed to adopt to survive in a marriage
with an overbearing, sick woman.

My aunt died three years later. I wasn't angry at her for
leaving. Her death certificate said, "acute alcoholism."
That's a tidy term for a slow and debilitating death. From
the time I was a teenager, Pearl and I enjoyed a warm and
affectionate friendship when she was sober, but I had
learned early-on in life to avoid her when she had been with
a bottle. Her whole personality changed. In her later years,
particularly after J. B.'s untimely death, Pearl was drunk
more often than she was sober. Alcohol had poisoned her
mind. She became paranoid, bitter, and vindictive.

When she became ill, it was my habit to go sit with her
every day at the hospital. Charles and I hired a nurse to
attend to her at night. She was a wise old woman,
uncertified but with a lifetime of bedside learning. I will
never forget the young doctor who was assigned to Pearl.
One night I tried to get some indication from him of her
prognosis. He looked at me from behind thick glasses and

said, "She could go on like this for six months. We just don't know."

I went in to squeeze Pearl's hand good-night. The old black nurse came in, took one look at my aunt's body that tremored with her belabored breathing, and said, "Honey, you bet' not go home tonight. She ain't gonna see morning. You see that kind of breathing she's doing? That's called chain-stoking. They don't have long when they start that." I trusted her judgment and called my mother, who was watching the children, to let her know that I wouldn't be coming home that night.

Before I could hang up the phone, the RN from the hospital staff hurried in, saying, "That's it. Get Kay out of here, she's passing." That seemed so strange. Here someone was dying, and they wanted me to leave? I refused. My instincts told me that my aunt needed me there even if it was going to be emotionally traumatic for me.

I sat by the bed and held her hand during the four to five minutes it took for her to pass. I just kept telling her, "It's okay. It's okay." I wanted her to know that I forgave her for all the jibes and anger she had directed at me in her alcoholic state. "It's okay," I whispered.

I sat with her, holding her hand, and watching her slip away. Seeing her laboring to leave this life left me with no sentimental feelings about the dying process. She didn't pass quickly. The downward physical spiral that began in her thirties accelerated near the end, but it was neither quick nor painless.

The night that she died was the first but far from the final step in a long and emotionally draining healing process that I went through to resolve the conflicting emotions I felt about my surrogate mother. The night that she passed wasn't an appropriate time to be angry. It was a time for forgiveness and reconciliation. It was a time to be magnanimous.

Eventually I had to own up to the emotions that were not pretty or nice that I felt towards my aunt. It wasn't until many years later when I was processing through the roots of some of my negative personality traits that I began to acknowledge some of the anger and resentment I felt towards my aunt for having emotionally and verbally abused me throughout my childhood. In the past decade or so, volumes have been written about the problems and stresses afflicting adult children of alcoholics, but when I was sorting through the relationship, I thought that it was just I who dealt with guilt, perfectionism, insecurity, and a high need to please.

Living with my aunt meant that no matter what I did, it was never enough to please her or win her approval. She never recognized my accomplishments. As an adult, I was angry that she never acknowledged that I really was a good person.

They say that the same sun that melts the butter, hardens the clay. During my childhood, certain things had been as constant as the rising and setting of the sun. My father's neglect, my aunt's alcoholism, loneliness. The heat of poverty, abandonment, racism, and the emotional abuse from my aunt could have made me very soft and needy, or very bitter and hard. I melted. I spent all of my life trying to prove to my aunt that I wasn't the "bitch or whore" she called me. And I still catch myself trying to do that as I try to please and win approval. I've spent most of my adult life trying to learn what made me react with softening rather than hardening. It's still a mystery.

I think that the Lord really wanted me to deal with those repressed feelings of anger and rejection before we left Richmond. They sure enough came to the surface when I discovered that, shortly before her death, Pearl had rewritten the formal will that she and J.B. had drawn up with their lawyer, Douglas Wilder. The second will was scrawled out in nearly illegible handwriting. In it, she handed out her possessions to her sisters, friends, neighbors, the milkman, and to all sorts of folks. J. B.'s sister Laura and I, the two main beneficiaries of the formal will, stood to lose over $100,000 if the second will was probated. I took both wills to my cousin, Oliver Hill, a very well respected attorney. His word was gospel. Whatever he said, we would do. He said that legally, as the executor of the estate, I could probate either will. I decided that, even if she was drunk when she rewrote the will, if she didn't want me to have it, I didn't want anything. I probated the second will.

It took a good couple of years to work out all the details of handing out Pearl and J. B.'s belongings and funds to all the parties that Pearl had promised something to. Like most families, we had to deal with squabbles and hurt feelings and greed that so often follow in the wake of a death. They had given me the house I had grown up in, which I cherished.

I should add as a footnote, that in the strange irony of life whereby God often finds a way to turn a sacrifice into a blessing, that house turned out to be quite an investment. It was just one year after we moved in that Charles was offered a position in Washington, D.C. We thought that it was shortsighted to turn down a chance to expose the kids to the sights and history of the nation's capital. So we decided to move to northern Virginia.

Housing was so much more expensive up north that with our meager savings we realistically could not have afforded anything outside of a trailer park. So, against the advice of all of our friends and relatives, we sold the house in Richmond and put the whole $62,000 we got from the sale as a downpayment on a house in Northern Virginia. Our older and richer friends tried to talk us into investing some of the money, but Charles and I knew that if that money were accessible, it would be spent. As it turns out, the housing market has done so well that the income and equity we've earned from the house far exceeds any earnings we could have conceivably gained from the cash given to me in the first will!

chapter eleven

AMAZING GRACE

"B I Z Z I E, S I T D O W N! Put your seat belt on!" I was getting exasperated.

"How can Jesus come in your heart?" asked our three-and-a-half-year-old daughter, Bizzie. Good question. Sometimes we repeat the Christian clichés so many times that we forget the significance of the words. Bizzie, her older brother, Chuck, and I were in the car running an errand. Can you think of a better place to do theology?

"When we say 'come into my heart,' we mean that we've asked Jesus to help us live the way that God wants us to and to stay with us all the time. Bizzie, Jesus wants every single one of his children to follow him. Do you want to ask Jesus into your heart?"

"You ask him for me." That was so typical of Bizzie. I had tended to do things for her that she was able to do and should be doing for herself. Well, not this time.

"Bizzie, when you decide that you love Jesus and want him to be with you always to be Lord of your life, and you want God to forgive you for the bad things you've done—then *you* have to ask him."

After a few rare moments of quiet, Bizzie started

singing again her favorite Sunday-school song: "Ho-Ho-Ho-Hosanna, Ha-Ha-Ha-Hallelujah, He-He-He-He saved me, I've got the joy of the Lord." I joined in with her. "I've got the joy, I've got the joy, I've got the joy of the L-o-r-d!" We were all giggles by now.

"I asked him," she said through giggles.

"Asked who, Bizzie?" I understood what she said, but I was more interested in what she meant.

"Jesus," she said. "I want him to be my Lord and live in my heart."

That simple declaration of faith came back to me as a reassuring blanket the night a few months later when I stood beside Bizzie's hospital bed and saw her heart monitor fall to a flat line.

• • •

Thanksgiving meant for us, as it does for so many families, a gathering of aunts, uncles, grandparents, cousins, and all sorts of James kin. To our children, it was more anticipated than birthdays, Easter, or the Fourth of July. It was second only to Christmas. Thanksgiving meant going to see their "Roanoke granny" and "Roanoke grand-daddy." It also meant no spankings for at least three days, all the sugar and junk food that their little tummies could hold, staying up late, no naps, getting to run inside, having stories read to them in a warm lap whenever they wanted, seeing Dad's baby pictures, hugs from relatives they didn't know, fights with their cousins, all the hugs and kisses they could possibly need, and a three-and-a-half-hour picnic in the car on the return trip home.

Preparing for this trip to Roanoke was more exciting than usual. I was going to be introduced to Robert Errington James III. My husband's grandparents were from Knoxville, Tennessee, and they had never seen their five-month-old great-grandson.

"Chuck, dial your dad's number for me and then hand

me the phone, please." I couldn't dial and nurse at the same time.

"What comes after 772?"

"I whispered the last four digits for fear of startling a drowsing baby. Chuck shoved the phone under my chin and dashed back to his room to continue stuffing books, toys, and undescribable treasures into a bag to take to Roanoke.

After a few moments I heard a click and Charles's voice, which sounded as though it were coming out of a tunnel.

"Hi. You ready to go?" he said gently. "Kay, are you there?"

"You know that I won't talk to you as long as you have me on that speaker phone." (I always felt as though the entire office was listening in. That's still true today.) I heard a click and there were no more ocean sounds in the background.

"Is that better?"

"Much."

"How's Bizzie doing? Is she going to be okay for the trip?" I wished that his voice had a bit more compassion in it when he asked that question. Charles and I were beginning to feel a bit of tension about Bizzie's constant low-grade fever and sniffles. He felt that she was fine, that seeing all of her relatives would do her good and maybe even help her kick this persistent flu. I had my reservations. During the day Bizzie seemed perfectly normal, but at night her temperature shot up so high that she became delirious. Trips to the pediatrician had turned up the often-heard advice, "A lot of this sort of thing is going around. . . ." "We're going to put her on antibiotics . . ." and "Call if it gets much worse." Much worse? If only the doctor had seen Bizzie at night, her sheets drenched with sweat, mumbling and crying that her head hurt. But in the end I gave in. Thanksgiving was such a family event.

The week that we came back from Thanksgiving Bizzie got much worse. We decided to pull out the sofa bed in the

living room, and I slept out there with her. Her fevers
spiked up to 103° and 104°. During the day her temperature
would drop and she appeared to be dramatically better.
Nights were filled with anxiety and tension, but at daybreak
she'd be perky and coherent, and we'd tell ourselves,
"Maybe she's going to be okay." After one particularly bad
Saturday night, I was in a panic. I felt my little girl slipping
out of my reach. Charles wanted to wait until after church
because he had responsibilities as an elder that morning. I
couldn't wait. We dropped him off at Stony Point, and I
went straight to the doctor's office.

"This is not the flu!" I practically yelled at the doctor.
"You've got to find out what's going on! This has gone on
too long." He finally agreed. Bizzie was admitted to the
hospital to run a series of tests. The doctor explained to me
that the testing is sort of like a funnel. He would run general
tests to see if he could narrow it down to a particular
disease.

I was distraught beyond comfort, and Charles was in
denial. "Everything's going to be fine," he kept saying. I
packed up a suitcase of Bizzie's things, and a friend, Valerie,
drove Bizzie and me to the hospital. Charles went to work.
Valerie understood the importance of distracting me in the
midst of a stressful time like this, and she put the radio on,
and we laughed and sang songs on the way to the hospital.

I started a vigil beside Bizzie's bed, but fortunately a
friend from church was wise enough to ignore my silent
pleas to be left alone in the room with my sick child, and she
pulled up a chair beside me. It was Ruth Wall, and Ruth had
an amazing ability to needlepoint and talk at the same time.
There were times when my emotions nearly overwhelmed
me and Ruth would engage me in conversation. It drove me
nuts until I realized what she was doing. She was keeping
me occupied so that I wouldn't dwell on the misery of the
situation.

That began a routine. Every morning I went to sit in
Bizzie's hospital room, and every day Ruth came to sit
beside me. My mother had come to take care of the boys,

who saw very little of their parents. At first I tried to keep up with nursing Robbie, but as the days wore on I realized that would be impossible. We had given up on family dinners at home at this point. We grabbed fast-food meals until money began to be tight. Then we started surviving on hot dogs and canned spaghetti.

Bizzie was admitted to the hospital on December third. Within three days I realized that Bizzie was slipping away from us. My bouncy and playful child was alternately lethargic and aggressive. She was going through long periods during which she was incoherent and didn't seem to recognize those in the room with her. She rarely spoke, but when she did it was like a broken record: "Mommy, I'm cold. Mommy, my head hurts." But I was helpless. The doctors couldn't diagnose her illness, and since they did not know what was wrong, they couldn't treat her. I began spending nights at the hospital.

Charles, who had been trying to convince himself that Bizzie really wasn't sick, finally had to face the truth. All of her charts and all of the looks on the doctors' faces told us that she was dying. Every day she lost another function, another sign of the life within. First she stopped walking, then she stopped eating. Then she slept all the time. These were the visible clues that she was slowly dying. There were invisible clues as well. Her internal system started shutting down. Her breathing and heartbeat became labored and irregular. Finally, she slipped into a coma. Once he was able to admit the awful truth that he might soon lose his only daughter, Charles snapped into action. He became the loving, supportive husband I needed. He took over the night shift, sleeping in a chair by her bed all night and working all day. After several days of this routine, we were both ready to be hospitalized for exhaustion.

Bizzie celebrated her fourth birthday in her hospital bed. The nursing staff sent up a little birthday cake and tied balloons to some of the machines that surrounded her, but by this time she had no idea what was going on around her. Charles ended up eating her cake for dinner that night.

Later that day I sat outside in the waiting room. I had gotten to know some of the other parents with children in the unit; we shared a sort of tragic bond. I remember coming out of Bizzie's birthday party completely devastated. In the hall I passed a woman and her daughter who was slowly walking with the help of a walker. They were smiling and laughing and enjoying each other's company. The little girl had leukemia. *You are so lucky,* I thought to myself in a sigh of self-pity. *I would give anything to trade places right now! At least you can laugh. You can hold your daughter and comfort her through the pain. You will at least be able to tell her you love her one more time before she dies.* What small consolations I sought.

Dr. Bundy, Bizzie's pediatrician, thought that perhaps the root of her illness was in her respiratory system. One of the top respiratory pediatric specialists in the country was a medical-school friend of his and happened to be in Williamsburg at a conference. Dr. Bundy persuaded him to come up from Williamsburg to look at this mysterious case he had. Charles and I were in the room when he came in to examine her. He had already studied her charts, and his examination was over in two minutes. "She's got tuberculin meningitis," he declared. My heart leaped. We finally knew what was wrong with her!

"What do we need to do? How bad is it?" we asked, full of hope.

"It's pretty bad. When the disease runs its course, it's usually fatal within three weeks," he said and walked out the door with Bizzie's charts. My heart sank. This respiratory expert was one of the coldest men I had ever met in my life. He held out no sign of hope, no consoling words. Just the facts. Three weeks.

His diagnosis brought a measure of relief. At least now we knew what we were dealing with, and we knew specifically how to pray. But we also felt dread at a disease that was so devastating. We searched our minds to try to figure out where she might have contracted it. Basically, tuberculin meningitis is tuberculosis that instead of settling on the lungs as it usually does, settles instead on the brain covering. So it wasn't in her lungs, it was in her brain—but she had contracted tuberculosis. "Where does a child get tuberculosis?" we asked ourselves. The doctor said that her illness really did begin with a cold, and as a result of her body's being run down by the cold, the tuberculosis virus that she'd evidently been carrying could take over because of her weakened condition. They said that she could have contracted the disease as much as six months earlier.

After we figured out what it was, we decided that we had neglected the boys for far too long. Robbie was six months old and had gone from being a nursing baby one day to a formula-and-bottle baby the next. I'm sure that it was a very traumatic experience for him. Chuck hadn't spent any quality time with us in three weeks. We didn't know how we were going to do it, but we made the decision that we were going to try to eat a homemade dinner with the boys every night. In addition to the pain I felt in association with what Bizzie was going through, I realized that we had two other children who were being neglected. The house was a mess. There was nothing in the refrigerator except limp celery, curdled milk, and a package of hot dogs.

It was during this period that I learned that one of the worst things you can say to someone in distress is, "If there's anything I can do, let me know." Never say that to someone in distress. First of all, he or she is too stressed to know. And people are hesitant to articulate what their real needs are anyway. A wise woman in our congregation realized after the diagnosis came that we were in for the long haul. She designated herself as the person we could call to make known our needs. By doing that she saved us the embarrassment of saying to those who called, "Well, we don't have any money for food," or "I'd rather be at the hospital than cleaning the bathrooms at home," or "We need someone to watch the boys next Tuesday from nine to one." Friends who wanted to help called her, and she assigned them a specific task.

That is how we survived. We worked with our

insurance and with others who were willing to contribute what the insurance didn't cover. We hired a private-duty nurse to stay with Bizzie at night so that we could sleep at home with the boys. Someone from the church loaned us a car so that I could get to and from the hospital.

One evening we were preparing Bizzie for the night nurse and straightening out her bed, and Charles noticed that her sheets were wet. Evidently, she had wet the bed after she slipped into a coma. As he reached to move her legs, we were shocked to notice they were as stiff as a board. I lifted her foot and her entire body came off the bed. We realized that she was having a seizure. Charles pushed the emergency bell and called for a nurse. I ran out into the hall to meet the nurse, and we came back in the room together. She took one look at Bizzie and then looked up at her heart monitor with a gasp. It was a flat line. My baby's heart had stopped. All heaven broke loose. The emergency heart team wheeled their cart into the room and pushed us out the door. The hospital chaplain, a Catholic nun, was on hand almost as fast as the resuscitation unit. She walked us out of the room, explaining that they needed all the room they could get to try to resuscitate Bizzie. The three of us walked numbly down the hall to the waiting room.

Pat Soehl, our friend from church who had gotten us involved in the Crisis Pregnancy Center, came into the waiting room then. He immediately figured out what was happening and called the church from a phone in the lobby. Within fifteen minutes our pastor, Reverend Frank Crane, was there with us. The four of us prayed until the resuscitation team came out of the room. Of course we all looked at Dr. Bundy's face to see if it was over.

"I'm sorry," he said, "This was unanticipated. We have been able to stabilize her, but she cannot stay here. It's very important to get her to the Medical College of Virginia. I think you might want to go see her before we move her." I could discern that Dr. Bundy was still afraid that we could lose her at any minute. He tried to prepare us for what we would see when we went back into the room. "She's not going to look the same," he warned. He described all of the various machines and tubes that had been inserted. He explained that they had ripped her clothes off her and that she was spread-eagled with something attached to every arm and leg.

Nothing could have prepared us for what we saw. She was a horror picture. Her head was shaved and she had a metal shunt stuck in her brain.

I asked Dr. Bundy if she could hear us. "Hearing is one of the last senses to go. If anything, she can hear you." I tried to think of what I would say to her. I thought back to our conversation in the car a few months before, and the most comforting thing I could think of to say was that Jesus was with her and that he would be with her forever. "Jesus will never leave you," I whispered in her tiny ear. "Nothing can separate us from God's love. Nothing."

All eyes turned to Charles, who turned to the nun and whispered something in her ear. She flew out of the room. "Uh, Mr. James, we really need to move Elizabeth. Time is of the essence." It was one of the twenty or so doctors and technicians crowded into the room. Tension hung in the antiseptic-smelling room. The rescue squad was anxious to transfer Bizzie to MCV.

"Nobody is going to touch my daughter until I pray for her," he said firmly. The nun returned to the room breathless, with a bottle of oil that she gave to Charles. Pat, Frank, and Charles anointed her with oil and prayed for her, each laying a hand on her lifeless body. We stood aside and they took her out.

Later that night at the new, better-equipped hospital, her new team of doctors sat us down and prepared us for the worst. "She's alive," they said, "but we don't know what the quality of her life will be even if she survives." They told us that her brain had been without oxygen, and it had taken sufficiently long to revive her—that we were probably looking at severe brain damage. "My daughter's a vegetable," I mumbled to myself. Charles and I didn't talk about what the doctors had said. I think we needed time to process through the heavy news on our own. We were physically drained. That night I began to feel intense physical pain as part of the grieving process. It was too much to bear. "If she's going to be in a wheelchair and a vegetable, then she'd probably be better off dead," I concluded.

Joyce Ranson came to the MCV waiting room that night. She wept as I told her the latest about her namesake, Elizabeth Joyce James. Tears streamed down my face as I confessed to her that I didn't know how to pray for Bizzie anymore: Should I ask God that she live even if it meant that she'd be physically impaired for the rest of her life? Should I be praying for a quick death to end her suffering?

Joyce sat bolt upright at that. "Listen here, young lady," she snapped, her eyes igniting, "I am asking God to heal her and to grant her life. Sweet, irreplaceable life. If Bizzie comes through this ordeal physically or mentally handicapped, she is still your daughter, and we will still celebrate her life." In the providential timing of God, Joyce had just returned from a conference on the sanctity of life. She warmed my heart with testimonies she had heard from those labeled unlikely to enjoy a "good quality of life." She told me about autistic adults, paralyzed children, and disabled men and women whose joy and enthusiasm for life was intact even if their physical or mental capacity was impaired. I found myself nodding. Then Joyce took my deepest fears head-on.

"Even if Bizzie were to continue on in a coma, unable to respond to our love and care, she is still our Bizzie."

• • •

There's a line from the movie, *Steel Magnolias*, that I've carried around with me since seeing the movie. "My favorite emotion is laughter through tears," one of the women says. During the next two weeks that Bizzie lay motionless, time and time again I experienced laughter through tears. I sat by her bed and relived some of our times together. "Bizzie, do you remember when we learned to bake biscuits together? We started throwing flour at each other, and the next thing we knew the kitchen was covered in a layer of white dust!" I'd giggle and think of another time we had spent together. "Oh, Biz, I'm just remembering our trip to the beach . . . " It was a one-way conversation; she never responded, not even an eyelid flickered, but a friend had told me that sometimes when children are in a coma, their mind is lucid and will dwell on memories provoked by conversation. I can remember thanking God over and over that we had made the decision to sacrifice financially so that I could stay home with the children. By the grace of God, as I sat at her bedside anticipating her death, I had no regrets about the childhood we had provided. I thanked God as I sat by her bed that I never ran out of stories and memories of our times together.

We had sort of forgotten about Christmas. It was intentional forgetting, I suppose. It just didn't seem right to be celebrating and singing carols, with Bizzie so sick. It was three days before Christmas and our house had no tree, no decorations, and we hadn't bought any presents because we had no money. Again, the church body rallied around us. I came home one night from the hospital, dead tired and depressed, and the entire house was awash with red velvet ribbon, pine boughs, and angels. The youth group had bought a tree and brought it over and decorated it for us. There were presents underneath for everyone in the family. Chuck was thrilled, I cried, again, and Charles stared misty-eyed at our transformed house. The Christmas spirit began to infuse our spirits in spite of the circumstances.

I was hanging out in the hospital corridor a few days before Christmas when the nurse came looking for me. She wore an intense look. My stomach knotted up. "Is this the end?" I wondered. Sensing my fear, she broke into an uncharacteristic smile. "I want to show you something." I practically ran to Bizzie's room. She lay in her bed snuggled next to her blanket. "Watch this," said the nurse, snatching Bizzie's blanket away from her face, laying it just outside her fingers. Bizzie grabbed it back. I almost fainted. Her eyes were still closed, she still seemed lost, but she had moved!

"Bizzie . . . Honey . . . Biz!" I called. Her eyes flickered open. "Where's my mommy?" she asked.

"Here I am," I laughed through tears. "Here I am, baby!" And I kissed her dry, cracked lips. She looked confused. I held her tiny, frail hands as she looked around the room taking in her surroundings. She looked at all the tubes and wires coming out of her body. She felt her bald head. Then she turned to me and said, "Can I have some peanut-butter cookies?"

I climbed next to Bizzie on her bed and pulled her close to my heart. We rocked back and forth and I whispered, "Thank you, Lord. Thank you, Lord," until I was hoarse.

It took me three tries to get the dime into the pay phone. Finally I got Charles on the line and told him that our daughter had "come back" and that she wanted some peanut-butter cookies, and that I was going home to bake them. He thought this was a great idea. We'd meet back at the hospital. Everyone else thought I had flipped.

"Kay, we'll go make some cookies for her. You stay here." "Don't you think she'd rather have some apple-sauce?" the nurses asked. No way. My daughter had been in a coma for two-and-a-half weeks, she had come back to us, she wanted my peanut-butter cookies, and she was going to get them! I was a wild woman. Back at home I had the phone under my chin letting everyone know the good news as I stirred cookie dough with my hands.

As soon as the first batch was done, I carefully wrapped them in a Christmas box and raced the car back to the hospital. I mean—I literally raced. A cop pulled me over for speeding. I offered him a cookie when he leaned in my window. "No, thank you, ma'am . . . Do you know how fast you were going?" he asked wondering at my tears.

I explained. "My daughter has just 'come back' and she's at the hospital and she wants peanut-butter cookies. And I'm bringing her my peanut-butter cookies so she can eat!" I exulted. He let me go.

"Just be careful so that no one else ends up in the hospital," he said, getting back in his car.

It was a glorious next couple of days. All of our friends from church who had been so helpful throughout the ordeal rejoiced with us in our good news. But the doctors cautioned us that she wasn't out of danger yet. Although she was recovering from the tuberculin meningitis, she was still very weak. The medicine she was on suppressed her immune system, making her very vulnerable to other infectious diseases.

Over the next several weeks, there were many ups and downs, but eventually the day came when she was released from the hospital. Her muscles had atrophied to the point that she couldn't walk, crawl, or even hold her head up. A long rehabilitation process began. We didn't know if any long-term physical impairments would linger. I guess we knew that the horror was over one day in March. I had bundled her up and set her on a lawn chair out front so that she could watch her brother ride his bicycle. Knowing that she couldn't move, Chuck teased her by getting on her tricycle and peddling down the driveway. I shook my head at my son's cruelty as I watched from the picture window. To Chuck's amazement, Bizzie pulled herself off of the lawn chair and onto the grass. She slowly and painfully pulled herself upright, walked down the driveway, and popped Chuck right on the nose. Then she got up on her tricycle and slowly peddled it back up the driveway. She angrily bundled herself back up and sat down on the lawn chair.

A year later Bizzie was completely recovered. Her hair grew back. She grew in strength. Her scars faded. But not all. Nor did our family lose all its scars. Some of the "scars" we carried with pride. They were like nicks and cuts in the growth rings of trees, marking years that brought seasons of drought and pain and exceptional growth. They were symbols of richer lives, of deeper understandings. One bedsore on Bizzie's heel became badly infected. It formed a callus and then a deep scar that is still with her today. We call it her "ebenezer." In Old Testament times, the people of

God would build a pile of stones to indicate the places in their lives where God had performed a miracle. When their children and others saw the pile of stones, called an *ebenezer*, they would naturally ask what the symbol represented. It provided the believer with an opportunity to give a testimony of the act that God had performed.

A look over Charles's journal from that time reveals the profound transformation in our view of life. We understand how fragile life is, how precious. And worth fighting for.

We also learned how essential the right kind of support is from friends and family. I still wonder how we ever would have made it without all the practical help volunteered by members of our church. Money would mysteriously appear in the mail box. Various small-group Bible studies committed to praying for our needs. One group prayed specifically for Charles. One group prayed for the boys. One group was lead to pray for Bizzie's long-term emotional and psychological well-being. It was interesting to me that without consulting one another, every group focused on a different aspect of our family's need.

Many well-meaning Christians offered a cheerful, "Have faith, believe that God will heal her." I understand their need to say something positive to us, but I believe that kind of "faith" is an affront to God. It is conditional faith. It is "faith" that God, like some genie in the sky, will let us back him into a corner with our demands. He has not called us to believe in his ability to bring about our desired outcome, whether it be providing us with a desperately needed job, healing our child, or helping us win a presidential election.

Our ordeal with Bizzie taught us what so many others in similar circumstances have learned: We are called only to have faith in our Lord Jesus Christ. To trust all that we have and all that we are into his care. Throughout the spiritual and emotional ups and downs of Bizzie's illness, we held onto his promise that "All things work together for good to those who love God, who have been called according to his purpose."

chapter twelve

WASHINGTON D.C.

SOMEWHERE IN BETWEEN the two-hour car ride from Richmond to the northern Virginia suburbs of Washington D.C., you cross a boundary more real in its effects than any state border. Yet you see no signs. It's an unofficial border, a separation in people's minds, some would say. But it's very real. It is the crossing from the porch-sitting, lemonade-sipping South to the hustle-bustle, here's-my-business-card North. The two regions have their own language. In Richmond, no word really had only one syllable. The first thing we noticed about northern Virginia were the variety of dialects that greeted us.

Living in the District itself would have put us in contact with many more black folks as well as with transplanted Southerners, but it was very important to us to maintain our Virginia residency. We dreamed that one day our children would go to college at one of the very good and very cheap Virginia universities. So we settled down in Annandale, Virginia, and consoled ourselves that it was only for a couple of years. Perhaps the biggest culture shock was the food. Our local supermarket didn't even carry chitterlings or pigs' feet, so occasionally Charles and I would get our soul-food fix at the Florida Avenue Grill in D.C.

Living in Annandale meant that I had a tedious seventy-mile round trip commute to and from my job every day. When I had gone in to resign from Circuit City in Richmond, I was given a promotion and assigned to the regional headquarters in Beltsville, Maryland. We were ecstatic! We knew that the cost of living meant that I would have to work, and now I had found a job without even looking! Working at Circuit City was an exhausting rough-and-tumble. It was a grueling pace, as anyone who works retail knows. The Christmas season began for me in October with the hiring of additional staff. Once November rolled around, even the management team hit the floor to sell and help the customers.

And then a fateful phone call. "Is this Kay James?" the unrecognizable voice asked. "Yes, it is," I answered politely, wondering who would be calling me at work. It was someone from the National Right to Life Committee. My stomach tightened. I just knew that they were going to ask us to temporarily house a baby and young mother. My job was wearing me down so much that I just was not in the mood to take in another baby and teenager. *Lord, no, no, no, no, please don't even let them ask, because you know that I can't say no.*

This time they had a different request. A black cable-television program was interested in doing a talk show on the abortion issue and how it relates to the black community. They wanted me to represent on the show the pro-life position. I laughed and said, "Thank you, but no—no way. Nope. But thanks for calling," and quickly hung up. They obviously didn't know whom they were dealing with. (I got sick to my stomach when it was my turn to read Scripture in Bible study!)

That night at dinner I told Charles and the kids about the unusual phone call that I had received. Chuck wasn't amused. About a month earlier we had been cleaning up the house, when he came across some of the pro-life literature we'd kept from our work with the Crisis Pregnancy Center in Richmond. He almost fainted when he saw the pictures of aborted fetuses in the pile. The way he looked at me, it was as if he had just discovered pornography in my closet.

"What are these pictures?" he asked with disgust. I felt weak. Think about it. How would you describe abortion to a child?—not, how you would defend it to an adult, or debate it before an audience, but *explain* it to a child? "Those are pictures of babies killed before they were born." He thought that that was the most incredible thing he had ever heard.

"Who would do such a thing?!" he demanded with obvious disgust. I tried explaining to him why women sometimes make that choice, but he wasn't buying any of it. He looked up at me and asked, "Why don't you and Dad make them stop?"

"We can't. What they're doing is not against the law." That startled him almost as much as the gruesome pictures. He couldn't believe that the country we had taught him to love condoned the killing of babies.

Then in his own child's way, he said, "Well, then, just change the law." I explained that every day there were people working to do just that. He looked disappointed. It was then that I promised him that given the opportunity I would do anything I could to help stop the killing of babies.

He reminded me of my promise that night at dinner. He looked up at me still giggling about the phone call and said, "But you promised." I stopped giggling. Charles suggested that I call them back the next day. And I did, hoping that they had found someone else. But they hadn't.

I figured that it wouldn't be all bad. It was a cable program and I was sure that it would run at two A.M. and that my mother and two other people would see it and that it would be no big deal. As it turned out, it aired live during prime-time. It was a nationwide show and took call-ins. To say that I was scared to death is an understatement. I hadn't slept the night before and I hadn't eaten all day. All I could think about as they hooked me up to the wireless mike was how awful it would be if I threw up in front of all those cameras and they caught the sound on my mike.

I debated a woman associated with Planned Parenthood. My opponent was a seasoned veteran, well-armed with statistics and polls. I felt like David going up against Goliath. There was no time to prep me for the debate. I went in with only the basic knowledge that I had received as a Crisis Pregnancy Center counselor. Despite my insecurity, the show went very well. I have since told people that to be effective in the pro-life movement, all it takes is a heart knowledge that abortion is wrong, genuine compassion for both women and children and a desire to help both, and obedience to the call of God in your life. That is all I went in there with that night. Based on audience response and the reaction of neighbors and friends who had seen the show, I won that debate.

I was just relieved when it was over. As they took off the mike that night, a sense of peace washed over me and the tension and anxiety that had haunted me ever since the phone call ebbed away. I also felt a bit of pride for following what I felt was God's call to speak out on the issue. Mission accomplished! I looked forward to falling back into anonymity in my role as mother and manager. But the Lord had other plans. Soon after the show aired, the Executive Director of the National Right to Life Committee called and asked to see the tape of the show. They had received hundreds of letters and phone calls in response to the show but hadn't seen it yet themselves. I invited the Executive Director and the Associate Director over for dinner, and they went in to view the tape on our VCR. They watched it through once and offered me a job on the spot.

"No, thank you very much," I said, getting their coats for them to leave. I had a wonderful job in corporate America that was allowing our family to live beyond the paycheck-to-paycheck just-scraping-by routine we had known our entire married life. The kids were in school, and Charles and I were beginning to enjoy the relaxed suburban lifestyle. Charles and Chuck both thought that I should do it, but the last thing I wanted was disruption in our lives.

One day a few months later, I was listening to a tape during my long commute to work. An Episcopal priest gave a compelling call to action to become involved in the pro-life movement. By the time I pulled into the parking lot at Circuit City, my carefully applied makeup was ruined from the tears streaming down my face. It occurred to me that while this battle for the lives of millions of unborn children was going on all around me, I could not hide myself behind a good job selling stereos and TV sets. Babies were dying because people like me didn't want to get involved. I called Charles as soon as I went into the office. He was ecstatic. Being an activist meant that I would take a tremendous cut in pay. Charles didn't care. He felt that I had some unique talents and gifts that were better used in the pro-life movement. It took three months from the time they came for dinner for me to pick up the phone and say that I wanted to join the team at the National Right to Life.

How could I ever forget my first day on the job? At that point I was still naive enough to believe everything that I read in the media about the pro-life movement. I expected the National Right to Life office to be staffed with dour white males in collars. But the very first person I encountered was a young black woman like me. She directed me to Doug Johnson's office. I walked down the corridors past the beautiful pictures of babies in the womb. There were baby pictures on every wall. Doug led me around to meet all the volunteers and staff. They were certainly very different from my colleagues at Circuit City. They were young and old, black and white, but they all had a special love and a warmth that reassured me. And I needed all the reassurance I could get.

The office had the frenzied pace of a campaign headquarters two days before the election. Phones were ringing, important looking people bustled by with anxious looks and reams of paper stuffed into their briefcases. I made a mental note to buy a briefcase. Everywhere I looked there were

women. Women answering phones, women running meetings, women plotting strategy against the backdrop of a map
of the USA. It reminded me of the frantic pace at the phone
company when we were swamped, but here the down time
never came.

I sat in on a meeting that first morning where they were
pulling together a press conference that I was going to
moderate! My head began to spin. *Dear Lord, what have I
gotten myself into?* My nerves got me so ill I had to go home
early. I felt like an overwhelmed kindergartner on the first
day of school. I cried in the shower the next morning, trying
to get up my nerve to go back. As soon as he saw me that
morning, Dan Donahey, the head of public relations for the
National Right to Life Committee, pulled me aside and said
that I would be conducting a press conference in front of a
major pharmaceutical company that day.

He must have seen the "I'm going to get sick" look
flash across my face. "Kay, don't worry," he soothed.
"You're a natural for this stuff."

"Yeah," I whined, "but you guys are pushing me into
the deep end of the pool!" To which he replied, "Maybe, but
you're a duck." I did the press conference and my nickname
became "Duck."

That began a whirlwind three years of debating, giving
speeches, holding press conferences, and traveling at home
and abroad almost nonstop. I was so busy doing, there was
very little time for learning. My briefings usually consisted
of a half page of notes given to me for the cab ride over to
CNN. I constantly felt ill-prepared and disappointed with
my performance. But the mail just kept pouring in saying
how my message had touched someone and either changed
or strengthened their position. A heartfelt mutual admiration developed between me and pro-lifers that I've enjoyed
to this day.

Events built to a crescendo in 1988. I began the year
with a three-week speaking tour in the United Kingdom.
When I returned to Washington, someone from Right to Life
told me they wanted me to go to one of the southern states

to endorse a pro-life candidate. I hopped right on another plane and headed south where I held a press conference endorsing a candidate I hardly knew. That proved to be a valuable lesson. We had just walked out of the press conference and were killing time in the hotel lobby watching television with the candidate. We had about fifteen minutes until we loaded up the car to drive across the state for another press conference. One of his opponent's campaign commercials came on while we were watching. It showed him at campaign rallies with several black people in the scenes.

"Jus' look at that! If I ran that stuff, I'd lose half maw base. Jus' look at him with those people!" our pro-life candidate drawled. I was stunned. This border-line racist is the man I just endorsed?! Needless to say, the next press conference was not the same glowing endorsement as the first. I muttered something like, "I'm here today to represent the National Right to Life, who wants to endorse this gentleman. Thank you very much," and I sat down. I never again endorsed a candidate without thoroughly checking out all of his or her views.

Right on the heels of that experience we covered the south for a round of Super-Tuesday press conferences. Then, without so much as a one-week breather, I hit the conventions of the state Right to Life chapters. My job was to mobilize the troops not only to vote but to become involved in the political process to help pro-life congressional, senatorial, and presidential candidates get elected. My travel schedule was so hectic that I was on the road more than I was home. And then the pace picked up! That summer I went to all three conventions: the Democratic National Convention, the Republican National Convention, and the National Right to Life Convention.

I was exhausted but exhilarated at the progress we were making. I knew that I was a success when Faye Wattleton, the formidable spokesperson for Planned Parenthood, refused to debate me. Whenever I was scheduled to oppose her in any forum, she backed out. One of my big

disappointments was when I went down to testify before
the Republican Platform Committee. Faye Wattleton and I
were to be on a panel together, and it would be my first
confrontation with her face-to-face. But she never showed.
Instead, she issued a statement for the record. That experience also proved to me a gut feeling I had had all along that
the media is solidly biased against the pro-life position. The
day after she didn't show on the panel, *USA Today* ran a
long story with her picture about how courageous Faye
Wattleton was to go into that forum and present her case,
knowing that she was not going to be successful. Courageous! She didn't even show up! The reporter wrote a
glowing story, oozing with admiration, and neither Faye nor
the reporter had even bothered to go to the event. How
courageous is it to back out and send a written statement? If
she was so courageous, then why was she afraid to face me
in a debate?

My most constant source of frustration while working
for National Right to Life, was the blatant and subtle
manipulation by the media on any news relating to abortion.
Even the talk shows like Donahue and Oprah were at the
bidding of the pro-abortion leadership. Once I was invited
to represent the National Right to Life on the Donahue
show, but Faye Wattleton told them that she wouldn't come
if I were on the show. So they un-invited me. Faye
Wattleton got to pick who her opponents were. They even
refused to allow me in the audience!

On another occasion, a woman in California was
charged with fetal homicide because her drug use had
caused her baby to be born dead. The media immediately
began asking for a response from the pro-life community.
We sat down and thought through what a caring and
sensitive response would be in a situation like this. Our
position was that the woman was wrongly charged for the
simple reason that she was a victim of a schizophrenic
society. She could have killed that baby any time up until
birth and not been charged with anything, but because the
baby was born dead, she was charged with fetal homicide.

Now, what the media wanted was an emotional, preferably judgmental, sound-bite from someone to splice into the evening news. We refused to give it to them. When the cameras came over to interview me for half an hour, only ten seconds of which I knew would be shown on the nightly news, I smiled nonstop and repeated over and over that the woman had been wrongly charged by a schizophrenic society that couldn't decide whether or not babies can be legally killed by their mothers.

The reporter jumped on that and asked me again and again about the "competing rights" of the mother and the child. That is a favorite trick of the pro-abortionists: to paint a picture of mothers against their infants. It is not women's rights versus children's rights as the media tries to spin it; not taking drugs is in the best interests of both the mother and the child. The reporter invoked images of "pregnancy police" who would go around and "make women not take drugs," or make women not drink a glass of wine or smoke a cigarette. She was provoking me, but I was determined to maintain my composure. They wanted a visual of an angry pro-lifer saying, "Throw the hussy in jail." But that was not our position at all. I glued a smile to my face and kept saying, "We believe that they are not competing rights but complementary rights."

We all anxiously gathered around the TVs to see what came on the evening news that night. Now the National Right to Life is indisputably the largest pro-life organization in America, representing the views of more pro-lifers than anyone else in the country, but because we wouldn't give the media the image that they wanted, they went elsewhere. The producer of that news story had already written the script in his or her mind; they were just looking for someone to say it. They found someone to say, "Throw the hussy in jail," and put him opposite the well-crafted and "compassionate" response of the pro-abortionists. Experiences like that really discouraged me because I knew that the uncommitted masses formed their views of the abortion debate from watching scenes like that one on the nightly news.

They never heard the views of the majority of the pro-life community; they were left to assume that all pro-lifers were as ignorant and judgmental as the characters the media found to interview.

Time and time again we would get calls saying, "We're doing a show on abortion. Can you get us someone with a collar?" And our office would say, "Our spokesperson is a black woman. She's very good. She'd be happy to do the show."

"No, no, no, we want a Catholic priest." They had already decided that that was how they wanted to portray the issue. They're looking for drama, controversy. No news editor wants reasoned, compassionate, articulate responses to the questions. They want entertainment.

For that reason, television and talk shows were always a frustrating experience. Debates, on the other hand, offered a bit more freedom to present our case. I have been told that I debate very, very well, but I am convinced that it is more the power of the message than the messenger. People respond when they hear the pro-life message in a calm and reasoned way. If I weren't so convinced of the value of debates, I would never have agreed to do them.

For weeks before a big debate I wouldn't be able to sleep or eat. I would be constantly on edge in anticipation of the trip, especially when I traveled to college campuses where I could expect highly antagonistic audiences. Fears clouded my thinking. Would I be able to respond to the points my opponent made? Would I forget everything when I saw thousands of eyes fixed on me in an unsympathetic stare? I felt enormous pressure to debate well; to be clear, creative, and concise. It is not an understatement to say that in the battle to forge a pro-life conscious America, millions of lives hang in the balance.

National Right to Life couldn't afford to send anyone with me on out-of-town debating trips. Those were some of the loneliest passages of my life. It was no fun traveling alone, debating without any staff support, and then having to return to an empty hotel room afterward. Whenever I was feeling particularly needy, I'd consider asking for someone to travel with me, but then I thought of all the grandmothers on fixed incomes who sent in their five- and ten-dollar checks, anything they could afford, to save babies. Most of our contributions were personal checks from families and individuals who gave sacrificially. So I went alone.

I'll never forget a debate at Princeton University against the past president of the feminist organization, National Organization for Women. My insides were in such turmoil the month before that debate that I actually gave myself ulcers. I always had a fear that I was going to go out and fall flat on my face. I just knew that they were going to bat a hard one at me and I wasn't going to know how to respond. Every debate was really a stretching out in faith, and I learned to trust God for wisdom and even for the very words I would speak.

I often joke with friends that I went into the movement a Presbyterian and came out some kind of Pentecostal. My prayer life changed dramatically. I had to learn to cry out to God. This was a routine I practiced before every debate: Two hours before we were due to go on stage, I would lock myself in my hotel room with the phone off the hook and "eat rug." "Eating rug" means to pray in the most humbling, miserable position possible—lying prone with your face down on the floor. From that vantage point I would confess to God my inadequacies and my fears. And I would ask him to speak his words through me.

During that time I would often meditate upon certain Scripture verses that emphasized the sanctity of unborn life. One of my favorites is a passage where the Lord tells Jeremiah:

> Before I formed you in the womb I knew you, and before you were born I consecrated you; I have appointed you a prophet to the nations.

As I read that before the Princeton debate, my eyes wandered down the page and I read Jeremiah's reply. "Ah,

Sovereign Lord! I do not know how to speak. I am only a child!"

And I said "Lord, that's me! That's what I feel like!"

I continued to read: "But the Lord said to me, 'Do not say I am only a child,' but you must go to everyone I send you to, and say whatever I command you. Do not be afraid of them, for I am with you and will rescue you." And I was hoping that meant literally, "Get me off that campus without getting lynched."

> Then the Lord reached out his hand and touched my mouth and said to me, "Now I have put words in your mouth. See today I appoint you over nations and kingdoms, to uproot and tear down, to destroy and overthrow, to build and to plant."

It was very comforting to me before I went out to do that debate, to know that the Lord had put his words in my mouth.

It was always a harrowing experience "preparing" for a debate, because I never planned out my responses. My best lines came to me on the spot—words I would say, given to me by God. I could never sit in an office and come up with the responses that came to me in the rush of a debate. For example, that night at Princeton, the moderator threw my opponent a real "softball question."

"Don't you think that adoption is an option both the pro-life and pro-choice movements can support?"

"Absolutely!" Judy responded. "Adoption is parenthood by choice. No one is being forced to care for a child that they don't want." And then she slipped into a sarcastic voice, "Can you imagine if the government pregnancy people knocked on your door and said: 'Open up, it's the pregnancy police— here's your child'?

"And you say, 'But I didn't order a child! I don't want one!'

"And they say, 'But you must take this child! The government wants you to have this child. You must raise and take care of this child.'"

Then switching to a sweet voice, she chided, "No one would approve of such a thing, and that's why I'm in favor of adoption, because adoption is parenthood by choice, and not parenthood by force."

And then they turned to me for my two-minute rebuttal, and I walked to the microphone thinking, "Oh, shucks . . . What am I going to say?" I didn't have a clue what to say, but when I hit the podium it came to me.

"Knock, knock, knock. 'Hello, I'm from the government and I have your child.'

'And you say, 'But I didn't order a child! I don't want a child!'

'And you hear, 'Oh, yes, you did. I have the paperwork right here. Nine months ago you signed a contract!'

'And you protest, 'But I didn't mean to!'

"Well, I'm sorry. Whether you meant to or not, here is the baby. What do you want me to do with it?'

"And you look at your child and say, 'Kill it.'

"That is what we're saying: You have a child. It is not forced pregnancy by the government; you have a child, but what you're forcing us to do—the rest of us in America—is to condone your killing your child because you don't want it." I turned to sit down without waiting to see the audience's reaction and they burst into applause before I even reached my seat.

The same debate, the question was posed to me (a hard ball—of course, our side always got the hard questions): "Don't you think that women need abortion in order to have economic parity with men in the work world? Men can't become pregnant, and therefore their careers are never interrupted by pregnancy, but women don't have that option. So to achieve economic parity with men, women need abortion services. How would you respond to that Mrs. James?" Aw, shucks . . . How was I going to respond to that? Again, it came to me as I reached the microphone.

"Say it LOUD! I am BLACK and I am PROUD! You know, back when I was in college, during the heyday of the black power movement, I learned that I didn't need a

Michael Jackson nose job, or to straighten my hair, or bleach my skin to be 'equal' to any white person. And I now know as a woman I don't need to be able to mutilate my body and kill my children to be equal to any man. The real feminists say, 'I'm pregnant and *you* better be prepared to deal with it!' I don't have to change anything about me to be equal to a man. I already am. And I don't have to change anything about me as an African-American to be equal to you. So the world better be prepared to deal with the fact that I'm black and I'm a woman, because I'm not going to change!" The audience roared.

And then I talked a bit about what real feminism is. Real feminism is saying "I am who I am. I don't have to change who I am to be equal to anyone. Why do I have to become like a man to be equal? I bear children; it is a part of who I am. And I don't need this 'right' to mutilate my feminine organs and kill my children in order to be equal to men. Maybe what we need to work on is getting the government and private sector to value women in their uniqueness, their strengths, and their needs, especially when they take on the role of mother. That to me seems a much more compassionate stance than killing their children."

After one debate I returned to my dark and lonely hotel room and called home. Robbie's six-year-old voice whined into the phone, "Mommy, why won't you come home?" He didn't ask why *can't* you come home, but why *won't* you? That was the beginning of the end for me. I decided that if I saved every unborn child in America and lost my own, I would have failed in my primary mission that God has called me to in life. It was time for me to slow down and spend more time with my family. I thought about working part time. And then came the heart-wrenching news that my mother was dying of cancer. I resigned from the National Right to Life.

• • •

My mother had been a servant all her life, constantly pouring out to others. Charles and I decided that even if it caused us to go in the hole, we were going to make her last few months the most glorious ones we could give her. We decided that I would temporarily move back to Richmond to care for her. Before I headed south, I stopped in at the Bush campaign office, which had switched gears after the election to a transition team. It was important for me to put in my two cents worth on a few issues close to my heart. When he heard that I was there, George Bush, Jr. stopped in to see me. We had gotten to know one another when I was campaigning for pro-life candidates, his father included, throughout the past year.

"Kay, would you consider coming on board?" he asked. I flashed him my "Come on now, be serious" look. "Really, Kay, you're a natural. Would you at least consider it?"

"No, I'm really not interested," I demurred, explaining that my mother had been diagnosed with cancer and the prognosis was not good. But it tickled me to have been asked. "How about that?" I asked myself getting into the car.

In her hospital room later on that day, I tried to encourage my mother before she went in for surgery. "You know, Mamma, I had an interesting offer today. George Bush, Jr. asked me to come in and serve in the new administration! Can you imagine that! Of course I said No, but it just tickled me that he would ask." Mamma wasn't smiling. Lying prone on her hospital gurney, minutes before she went in for surgery, she proceeded to bless me out as only a black woman can do.

"Girl, what's wrong with you! I raised you better than that! The son of the President of the United States asks you to serve your nation and you say no! How many people do you think get that kind of opportunity? How many black folks you think being asked?! Girl, you bes' get back on that phone and tell him you was just kidding!"

She made sure that I called campaign headquarters from her room. After they wheeled Mamma out, I told George that based on my skills and abilities, I wanted to come in as high as I possibly could "because I don't have a lot of time to make my mother proud."

A day or two later I got a call from Senator Orrin Hatch, who said that he wanted to introduce me to Dr. Louis Sullivan. Louis Sullivan, I knew, was an eminent researcher and physician well-known for establishing the Morehouse School of Medicine. We met. He was very impressive. A mutual respect developed. John Sununnu, the president's chief of staff, had already offered me a position in the White House, in the Intragovernmental Affairs division, but I decided to turn it down after Dr. Sullivan invited me to join him at the Department of Health and Human Services where he was to serve as Cabinet Secretary. I figured that it would be much more rewarding to use my skills and talents to help the only black member of the cabinet make his dream a reality.

Dr. Sullivan had quite a challenge before him. HHS has the fourth largest budget in the world, behind the national budgets of the United States, the former Soviet Union, and Japan. Agencies as diverse as the Social Security Administration, the National Institutes of Health, the Food and Drug Administration, and the Centers for Disease Control fell under his purview. HHS is also the department responsible for formulating governmental responses to such pressing societal problems as child abuse, runaway children, teen homicide, drug abuse, and welfare dependency. I thought to myself, *When the President talks about a kinder, gentler nation, this is where we're going to have to make it happen.*

I was so proud that I couldn't squeeze the smile off my face when I went in to tell my mother that I would be serving as the Assistant Secretary for Public Affairs at the U.S. Department of Health and Human Services. Mamma looked a little disappointed: "But you can't even type!"

I explained that it was a subcabinet position, an office with enough responsibility to require Senate confirmation. She smiled at that. We were both looking forward to her being able to witness my swearing-in ceremony, but the confirmation process took so long (politics has a way of throwing sand into the gears of government) that she was too weak to make the trip. She died four months later.

In the months before her death I spent every weekend in Richmond. We would go out walking together in the afternoons, usually at a nearby shopping mall, so that she could get some exercise and get out of the house. On one of our last trips, we were passing a window display and I fell in love with a heart-shaped Waterford crystal pen holder in the central display. I whined to Charles later that it sure would make a nice anniversary present. My mother, who had never spent a great deal of money in her life, sent the entire Waterford crystal desk set to me as a gift when I was finally confirmed. It arrived in the mail just a few weeks before her death. I think of her giving spirit every time I use it.

It was during this period that I became "Kay Coles James" instead of my usual Kay James. The reason was that several magazine articles and newspaper stories were being written about me, sort of local-black-girl-makes-it-big kind of stories, and no one would believe my brothers when they insisted that I was their sister. It was out of respect for my family and not any feminist zeal that I started including my maiden name in publications.

The role of Assistant Secretary for Public Affairs at HHS is one of the most challenging, interesting, and crucial assignments in the political world of Washington. It is an ideal assignment for a single person, or a married person without children or whose children are no longer at home. For a parent, a mother, with children still in elementary and junior and senior high school, it required an enormous amount of time and energy. We began the day with 8:00 A.M. meetings, and it was rare when I left the office before 7:00 P.M. at night. Even weekends were eaten away by out-

of-town trips and breaking stories. Instead of having the
"crisis of the week" we had the "crisis of the hour."

But in all fairness I have to admit that I knew what I
was getting into before I signed on the dotted line. When I
was serving on the transition team, the Chilean grape crisis
broke out and everything and everyone was thrown into a
frenzy. I can remember meeting late one evening with the
Secretary's senior staff to discuss the issue, and Dr. Sullivan
had to leave to attend a black-tie dinner. "We'll reconvene
here at 10:00 P.M.," he said, and no one batted an eye. It was
enough to give me second thoughts. Those 10:00 P.M. crisis
sessions flashed through my mind as I was repeating my
oath during my confirmation. I had a difficult time with the
line that I was accepting this job with "no mental reservations." I sort of mumbled that part.

It had been a grueling pace. The demands of my job
had just about strained all of our family relationships to the
limit. When my old friend, Doug Holladay, called about a
position with the nonprofit One-to-One Partnership, I was
ready for a break.

Ray Chambers, the man whose vision and dollars
created One-to-One, invited me to lunch at a restaurant I
had only read about in glossy magazines. He explained to
me over a wonderful lunch why he was investing his
resources and abilities into an organization like One-to-One.
His philosophy was that in order to reach at-risk youth, we
need more than programs and policies. We need to connect
them with consistent, caring adults as mentors. As a
successful businessman himself, Ray had a vision for the
positive and unique role that business executives could play
in reaching troubled kids.

As Chief Operating Officer, my primary goal was to
instill some basic management principles. In one sense, the
job was my worst nightmare. One-to-One was an unstruc-
tured, start-up organization high on vision and enthusiasm
and low on personnel, policies, and procedures to carry it
out. They had substantial resources but no computer
system. But in another sense, it was a dream job. I could

start at ground zero and build a solid organizational foundation. The pace was still hectic but it wasn't the frantic, time-consuming whirlwind of HHS. After a year I left One-to-One in the hands of someone who could advance it far beyond where I had taken it and once again plunged back into the world of politics as Associate Director of the Office of National Drug Control Strategy for the Bureau of State and Local Affairs.

This was basically a liaison position, something I had a good deal of experience with. In a nutshell, I would take the President's drug policy and interpret it at the state and local level and then reverse the flow of information to represent their views back at the policy table in the White House. It was surely a thankless, difficult post, but I had to fight for that thankless, difficult post. A few of the white, male, liberal Senators questioned my qualifications for the job during my confirmation hearings. While I certainly agreed with them about my lack of any formal drug-policy training, I reminded them that I was one of the few policy wonks in D.C. who grew up in a neighborhood, and in a family, under the siege of drug and alcohol addiction. My insights on substance abuse treatment, enforcement, and prevention came through firsthand experiences with my father and brother. I was confirmed. The kids dubbed me the "Drug Czarina."

And as I write this, I am recovering from the exhausting effort required in helping with President Bush's reelection campaign while continuing my work with the Office of National Drug Control Strategy. Yes, we lost, but it was a battle worth fighting. As I look ahead to the country's future as well as my own, I can't help but recall the brief speech I gave at the Republican National Convention. As I mounted that massive stage to speak about family values, I remembered my own family—certainly not the perfect Mom-and-Pop-with-two-sweet-kids-in-a-tri-level. But a family just the same. Even when it becomes fractured or damaged by the cares of this world, it is still the unit that was meant to give each of us a sense of who we are; of who we can become.

So to Mamma. Daddy. Aunt Pearl and Uncle J. B. To the many friends who became family and to my husband and my own children, I can only say: *Thanks*.

I will never forget.

chapter thirteen

HOW SHOULD WE
THEN LIVE?

T H U R G O O D M A R S H A L L was retiring. For decades he had been the voice for black America on the United
States Supreme Court. The Justice who replaced him would,
in many respects, represent the convictions of a new
generation of African-Americans, and the liberal black
leadership could not digest the possibility that the new
nominee may not be one of them. In a very real sense,
Clarence Thomas's confirmation fight was a battle for the
hearts and minds of the African-American community.
From corner stores to the McNeill-Lehrer Report, the
Thomas hearings sparked debate among African-Americans
about where we ought to be going and who should take us
there.

On one side of the debate were members of the liberal
black establishment: the leadership of the NAACP, the
Urban League, the Democratic Party, and the media elite.
Spurred by much-needed court victories during the civil
rights era, these leaders still looked to big government and
the courts to solve problems such as chronic poverty,
joblessness, family disintegration, drug abuse, and low
educational achievement.

On the other side of the debate were conservative voices from both parties who agreed with liberals about the severity of the problems but disagreed about the best strategy for solving them. Black conservatives trace their roots to the post-emancipation self-help movement, when freed slaves relied on faith, family, and the black community to overcome the obstacles in their path. While supportive of some government programs, black conservatives prefer individual efforts by the business community and church leaders. These efforts should be conceived and implemented by people who have the vision to rebuild our families and communities.

In short, one side speaks of rights, entitlements, and handouts. The other speaks of reciprocal responsibilities, opportunity, and empowerment. Conservatives can also be identified by their willingness to talk about the need for personal responsibility when issues such as illegal drug use, teen pregnancy, and the health-care crisis in America are raised.

Black conservatives are not a new phenomenom. Surveys have consistently shown African-Americans to be more socially conservative than their white counterparts. African-Americans are more likely to attend religious services, more likely to oppose abortion, and more likely to disapprove of illegal drug use and out-of-wedlock births. African-Americans also hold decidedly mixed views on racial-preference strategies such as affirmative action. Despite such diversity of opinion, African-Americans are often taken for granted as a monolithic liberal voting block. This illusion is strengthened by political and intellectual leaders who muzzle discordant views within the black community.

The intense lobbying against Clarence Thomas by members of the liberal black establishment is a prime example of an attempt to muzzle a voice. The ironic truth is, the race that for so long had to fight and die for the right to vote and think for themselves had submitted to a political orthodoxy where anyone who disagreed with the party line soon found his or her racial loyalty suspect.

A favorite tactic of black liberals is to accuse their conservative counterparts of forgetting where they came from. In my own experience, I have often been accused of forgetting my past. Both Charles and I, and even our children, have experienced this phenomenom. The charge is usually leveled by someone who doesn't think it's possible to be middle class, educated, speak standard English, and still be *truly* black.

During one abortion debate, a woman in the audience angrily told me I was obviously so middle class that I didn't have a clue as to the conditions that poor black women face. "If you realized what these women were going through, you would realize that abortion is their only choice."

I asked that woman to consider a poor black woman on welfare. She already has four kids and an alcoholic husband who has all but abandoned the family. Now she discovers that another child is on the way.

"How would you counsel that woman?" I asked.

Without hesitation, she answered, "The most compassionate thing that woman could do for herself and the children she already has is to have an abortion. If brought into this world, that child would have a very poor quality of life."

"I have a vested interest in your answer to that question," I responded. "That woman I described was my mother. I was the fifth of six children born into poverty. And in case you're interested, the quality of my life is just fine!"

My mother faced unbelievably difficult circumstances, but she has never lamented that abortion was not a "safe and legal" option for her. Quite the contrary. In her later years she felt blessed to be surrounded by her six children, loved and cared for by a daughter whom my opponent would have counseled her to abort.

I haven't forgotten the racial slurs, the spit in my face, or the pin pricks I faced when I integrated the schools. I haven't forgotten being turned away from housing simply because I am black. And I most certainly haven't forgotten my childhood and the pain of going to bed hungry and cold.

An I will never forget. I can't forget. *We* can't forget. We have too much proud history, too much experience in surviving this obstacle course called America to forget everything and start from scratch.

As I look back over my life as a metaphor for the survival of the black race in America, I see clearly that while government programs and court decisions played a major role in our advancement, so, too, did the sharing of key values that preserved our community: integrity, self-reliance, perseverance, family loyalty, and responsibility. If we are to make progress against the pathologies that plague our families and communities, these values must still play a leading role.

In addition, we must be willing to take a hard look at some of our own self-destructive patterns of behavior. Right now the biggest killer of young black males is young black males. The health statistics for black families are so poor it has become apparent that many black women are slowly killing themselves with a high fat, high salt, high sugar diet. Unfortunately, many liberals are afraid to talk about values and self-destructive behaviors for fear, I guess, of feeding the fire of racism.

For example, in the wake of the Rodney King verdict and the subsequent L.A. riots, representatives from the NAACP, the Urban League, and black academia availed themselves to reporters to give "the black analysis" of the riots. Their interpretations of events largely cast the looting and violence as the inevitable consequence of years of discrimination and poverty. Speaking for black America, they pointed their fingers at white America and declared that the rioters were justified in their actions because of eleven years of Reagan-Bush neglect. There was certainly no indication that perhaps broken homes, substance abuse, idleness, materialism, or greed had anything to do with the people of all colors who hauled away boom boxes, food, televisions, liquor, refrigerators, and anything else that wasn't nailed down.

How did this analysis go down with most African-Americans? While we all felt betrayed and tried to contain our righteous anger after the miscarriage of justice in the Rodney King trial, most African-Americans knew we were capable of pronouncing and displaying our anger in a productive manner. In a survey of 750 African-Americans sponsored by Home Box Office and the Joint Center for Political and Economic Studies, only eight percent said the rioters were justified in their behavior. Fifty percent said the rioters were unjustified but they could "appreciate how they felt and why they rioted"; thirty-seven percent said that the rioters "were not justified regardless of the verdict in the Rodney King beating." Thankfully, the citizens of Detroit demonstrated this during a similar tragedy involving police officers who beat a black man to death.

Clearly, the reigning liberal leaders of Black America are out of step with the values of most African-Americans. A similar "convictions gap" was revealed during the Clarence Thomas hearings. Poll after poll showed that while the liberal black leadership was denouncing Thomas, the majority of African-Americans supported his nomination.

The lesson to be learned by the L.A. riots and the Thomas hearings is *not* that conservatism should be the new reigning political orthodoxy of the black community but that it is time to allow the full range of values and views to be debated. And we should be able to conduct these debates, in barber and beauty shops as well as in political circles, without questioning one another's motives. The battle isn't about who cares the most for African-Americans. We shouldn't allow other people to pit us against each other, and we certainly shouldn't pit ourselves against each other.

There are too many children to be fed, jobs to be gained, families to be strengthened, and houses to be built for us to continue to waste time arguing about who loves and cares for black people the most. Ideas are popping up all over the country on how best to deal with our situation.

Some think that we should move toward greater government involvement, some think we should move away from government involvement. Some stress economic answers, some stress cultural and attitudinal change. I am "naive" enough to believe in the free market of ideas. As long as we "do no harm," we should test various proposals in communities across America. We ought to be secure and confident enough in our own ideas to not mind their being challenged. Unfortunately, these issues become highly politicized, and a lot of careers and money rest on the status quo.

For example, Polly Williams, who has been stopped at every turn by the ACLU and school officials, tried to initiate a voucher system in the Detroit Public School system. Under her plan, parents would be given a voucher that they could use to have their student attend any *public* school of their choice. School officials and Democratic legislators shot down the proposal for being "unfair to blacks," even though eighty-three percent of African-Americans believe that choice would "help poor children gain better access to a better education."

The same story is repeated with Kimi Gray, a public housing tenant and former welfare mother who is leading the fight to promote resident management of public housing facilities. The idea, championed by President Bush's Secretary of Housing and Urban Development, Jack Kemp, has been systematically opposed by the liberal black establishment. Yet ninety-one percent of blacks said they would support a program to allow public housing tenants to buy their units.

Ironically, neither Polly Williams or Kimi Gray would identify themselves as black conservatives. Ms. Williams was the Michigan state chairperson for Jesse Jackson's presidential campaign. And far from being the suburban, middle-class black who has forgotten where she came from, Kimi Gray, mother of thirteen, still lives in the inner city in public housing that she helps manage. These men and women represent a new and growing group of black leaders who are willing to challenge the traditional ways of thinking and doing things. And they are doing it by embracing "conservative" principles.

What are these principles? My list would include:

An emphasis on being a survivor, not a victim. We need to focus on what we can do, not what's being done to us. We have been too worried about "blaming the victim" when, in effect, we are "laming the victim" by convincing our youth that they have no control over their own destiny. They hear too often that their fate is in the hands of a racist society or sinister economic forces beyond their control. Such lessons breed passivity, helplessness and dependency, and finally, anger. We need to stop harping on the negative and celebrate the positive trends among our people. Confident youth, inculcated with the belief that they can achieve, are more likely to seize opportunities.

The key item in the black agenda should be to strengthen our families. It does not denigrate the hard work and the admirable job that single parents are doing to say that we need to encourage two-parent families. Research clearly shows that children raised without a father in the home are at a disadvantage financially, emotionally, psychologically, and physically. All policies and programs should be evaluated to ensure that they do not inadvertently weaken family formation and bonds.

Policies and programs, whenever possible, should be developed and implemented by private-sector, church, and community leaders. The goal is to empower parents and community leaders, not bureaucrats.

It is unfair to mortgage our children's future by burdening them with an astronomical debt. Both at home and in the Congress, we need to learn to spend only what we have and stop our credit addiction. At the same time, we cannot balance the budget on the shoulders of families struggling to make ends meet. We must allow families to keep more of their income by keeping their taxes low.

Any policy that ignores the central role of religion and morality in the healthy functioning of our society will fail in the long run. The strong religious character of African-

Americans is a strength and an asset, not a "personal matter" to be ignored.

Of course these principles would vary from person to person. I didn't develop my list overnight. It represents the culmination of a whole lifetime of experience and learning. It often occurs to me as I walk through offices in the White House, as I glance at the "power walls" filled with ivy-league degrees, lofty titles, and pictures with important people the office holder has known, that God raised me up to be a leader by giving me a slightly different preparation.

He began with a few lessons in humility in the slums of Portsmouth, Virginia, and then at Creighton Court in Richmond, Virginia. But the chill of poverty and alcoholism was warmed away by the love of family and neighbors who brought healing to a broken home. He blessed me with an extended family of kin and community who taught me right from wrong, and brothers who taught me pride in earning my way in this world.

Black educators imbued an expectation of excellence. In breaking the color barrier as a schoolgirl, I learned the evil of racial hatred. In college, God taught me to appreciate my heritage, to see that I was beautifully and wonderfully made. I graduated from college with the knowledge that I was his beloved child; it was the most important thing I learned in school.

He gave me a husband whose sense of humor through all life's trials taught me resilient joy. My daughter's brush with death taught me the sanctity of life. And he gave me the opportunity to use my gifts and talents to speak for those who can't speak for themselves: unborn children. Most of all, there was Mama, the black sheep of the family, who taught me through her life, the essence of love, the importance of family, and the meaning of faith.